From the Rose Garden of the Heart

When the Soul Soars

Robert Malouf

Contents

A Letter to Humanity

Dear humanity,
And for whom I have so much love,
I write this plaintive missive of the heart,
Humbly, respectfully,
And for your consideration:

I do not know
How cruel we can be,
I only know how cruel we are, how cruel we have been.

I do not know
To what depths we can sink,
I only know to what depths, already, we have sunk.

I do not know
The injustice we are capable of,
I only know the baneful injustice that is.

I do not know
The extent of our blindness to truth, our affection for lies,
I only know the willful blindness to truth that is.

I do not know
The harrowing despair the world will see,
I only know the crippling despair that is.

I do not know
To what cavernous depths of self-delusion we are capable of,
I only know the abysmal depths of self-delusion that are.

I do not know
How many masks of falsehood we will wear,
I only know the myriad masks of falsehood I have seen.

I do not know
When we will awake,
Arise to create the world that must be,
I only know
We must awake from the dark dreams
That are destroying us.

I do not know
Why we can not see the Light,
When, more brilliant than the sun,
It is all around us.

I do not know
When wars and hate and pride will end,
But, for your sake, dear humanity,
And for this I pray,
May it be soon!

A Light Uniquely Yours

From supernal heights
And bursting forth
From the firmament of justice and destiny,
Gleam forth in arrays of dancing,
Adorning light
The dazzling rays of womanhood
To illuminate the gifted, beauteous,
Rose-scented gardens
Of the hearts and minds
Of enlightened women
In homes and villages, cities and towns,
Great metropolises,
Places hidden, remote.

In this Day
And by the Pen of Truth,
These dazzling rays
Reveal gifts of spirit, mind and heart
Long denied, too vast to reckon –
Gifts carried in the womb of humanity
That now, irrepressibly,
Have come forth
Even as a babe comes forth from the womb
To grow, stand tall, be counted,
Leave its mark
On the scroll of life.

Women and girls,
So long bound by the shackles

Of effete traditions, veiled fear
And debilitating,
Illusory conceptions of inferiority,
Are now released
From the constraining, heavy chains
Of demeaning, deadly and destructive practices
That repress and suffocate breath and voice
Essential to eliminate the crushing cries
Of prejudice and injustice,
To realize lasting peace and true prosperity
And the long-promised
Well-being and happiness
Of all peoples.

Womanhood,
At last,
And after the passing of ages,
You have emerged in all your splendor,
A fiery, brilliant phoenix
Rising from the mire of centuries past,
Myths old,
To fly high and soar long,
Reach beyond the sky
To the realm of untold possibilities,
That you advance civilization,
Transform hearts and minds,
And assume your rightful place,
Celebrated protagonist on the global stage
With voice and lines
Unmistakably yours.

Womanhood,
Shine forth,
Ablaze

With light from on high!
Let its undying rays beam brightly
In the lantern of our times
With brilliant discernment,
Glowing wisdom,
Deep and true understanding,
Waves of oneness.
It is yours to illumine, as only you can,
Art and science, world affairs,
Family and community,
All human endeavor.

Womanhood,
Lover of peace,
Strong and resolute,
Táhirih your shining example,
Humanity in its essence
Is calling to you, pleading with you,
To respond to your high calling,
To shine forth
In dazzling rays and gleaming gifts
That an all-loving Creator
Has ordained uniquely yours,
Gleaming gifts of insight and cooperation,
Unveiled capacity and spiritual energies,
That your counsel be given,
Your voice heard,
That humanity neither falter nor fail
In achieving its true and glorious destiny
So long aspired to –
A world unified, glorious,
Reimagined,
A reimagined, glorious,
Unified humanity.

A Poet's Dream

One good line
To stand the test
Of time,
Is this too much
To ask
Of Thee,
O, Lord?

One clear thought
From Heaven brought,
Is this too much
To ask
Of Thee,
O, Lord?

One sweet rhyme
For every clime,
Is this too much
To ask
Of Thee,
O Lord?

And words so fair
That cause hearts to care,
Is this too much
To ask
Of Thee,
O, Lord?

And verse that stands
A thousand years,
To touch hearts
And draw tears
In love of Thee,
Is this too much
To ask
Of Thee,
O, Lord?

For Thee alone,
I raise my unworthy pen,
For Thee alone,
I struggle,
And fail,
To pen a line
Of beauty,
Or meaning,
To reach even
The remotest flames
Of Your lovers' hearts,
Or rise above
The drifting sands
Of this longing poet's
Impotent hand.

Ana and the Rabbi

Inspired by two dear souls

How loving these two
Perched high
On the branch of oneness,
Secure in the tranquil nest
Of God's love,
Abiding faithfulness.
How sweet their devotion
Smile by smile,
Glance by glance,
Their love and joy buoyantly alive
For all to see,
Find delight
In the light of their union
Ever-shining,
Never contrived.

How tender their affection
As they listen
With thought and care,
Mind and heart engaged,
Attentive, sincere,
That a tapestry
Of reflection and meaning
Be woven word by word,
Soul by soul,
On the loom of fellowship,
Insights and understanding.

How precious is love,
This greatest gift of all,
When unrestrained, freely shared,
Proffered without exception
To all who walk the path of search,
The broad avenues of life,
Who long to soar the supernal skies
Of truth and purpose.

How sweet these two,
Perched high
On the branch of love –
And how sweet their being,
Voice and visage,
Each and every
Thursday night!

As Birds Fly

As birds fly,
So may my heart.

As roses bloom,
So may my soul.

As warblers sing,
So may my life intone sweet song.

As spring gives life,
So does the Divine Springtime.

As birds fly
And roses bloom,

As warblers sing melodies sweet
And springtime brings renewal,

May my soul be alive
To the Everlasting Springtime
Of manifest Revelation.

Barren Sands

Barren sands
Of barren dreams,
Parched in searing winds
From times untold,
With broken shells
Of broken lives,
And hopes adrift
As scattered driftwood
Washed ashore —
Return to the Sea,
Where all is good
And life abounds,
Where calm dwells
In sacred depths,
And mighty ocean roars
Are but the voice
Of majesty and grace.

The Ocean calls,
How long must you wait?
Cool waters
In waves of love
Rush to you,
Why do you hesitate?
Whispering breezes carry your name
Illumined in sunlit letters,
Immerse yourself
In the Most Great Ocean,
Where beauty is fashioned

In shells of love,
And tides of hope
Move in crescendos
Of fulfillment,
Where barren sands die to self
To emerge as pearls,
Radiant,
Exquisite,
In their lustrous destiny.

Blind Man

Blind man,
Lend me your ear
That you might see.
Waves of splendor,
Oceans of light,
Flow from His Pen,
Rushing
For the shores of hearing,
The thirsty,
White sands
Of longing.

O friend,
Open your heart
To the mighty torrents
That spring
From the Beloved's breath.
Hear the sounds
And melodies
That stream
From His Hand.
Give them passage
To pulsate
Within the artery of your soul,
And flood
The chambers of your heart
With mystic meanings.

Then Vision,
Eternal,
Transcending dimension,
Illuminating,
Will brighten your path
To the All-Glorious Beloved,
He who waits patiently
At heaven's doorway,
The doorway
Of every seeking heart.

Brown Sugar

Sugar,
Brown, white,
Honey and molasses,
Dark and light –
All valued!
All sweet!

Roses,
Red, yellow, pink, white –
All fragrant!
All beautiful!

People,
Black, brown, tan, white –
All human!
All God's children!
All created in His image!

Humanity,
All peoples, all colors –
Let us learn
From sugar and honey, molasses and the rose,
That each person be valued,
Live a life of repose!

In such a world,
Just, united, gloriously diverse –
And, assuredly it will come! –
Will be heard from heart to heart

The following verse –
"All valued! All sweet!
All one human family,
At last!"

Butterflies Upon the Wind

Butterflies upon the wind,
Fluttering wings
Quietly proclaiming melodies
Windflowers love,
Melodies composed
In the rejoicing, pulsating
Heart of spring,
Melodies to accompany
Honey bees
As they go flower to flower,
Make honey
With the sweetness
Of springtime zephyrs
Romancing hyacinth and jasmine,
Wafting their redolence
Garden to garden,
Heart to heart,
Where they linger long,
Perfume love
And lovers;

Leaves rustling
Tales of mystery
To tease attentive ears,
Tales recited
On the outstretched stage
Of bough and branch,
Tales enchanting,
Beloved,

Their mystery held close
In the throbbing bosom of Nature,
Fair maiden
Crowned Queen of Creation
By the hand of God;

Warbling songbirds,
Enraptured by rose and love,
Unfolding mysteries of the heart
By day and night,
Mysteries calling poets to ponder,
Savants to unravel
Should they foolishly dare,
Mysteries heard,
Breathed in deeply
As they waft through sunlight
And moonlit nights,
Their beauty and mystery
Defying unfoldment by time
Or seeking heart,
Mysteries pondered
By thoughtful souls,
Mysteries that intrigue,
Unwilling to be solved,
Committed to the page
By the poet's hand –
Only wind and air
Can tell their tale,
Reveal their mystery,
Poetic beauty;

Breezes softly blowing
Harmonies

Quietly played
To enchant the soul,
Cause the love of lovers
To flower and bloom
As beauty flowers and blooms
In spring,
Harmonies played
On the strings of time
In the key of love and delight
That give voice
To pairing doves,
Meadowlarks,
The call
Of the whip-poor-will;

In all these,
Is it Thy voice,
O Unseen Beauty
Who dost breathe life
Sweet, undying, vibrant,
Into wind and breeze,
A voice that thrills my being,
Vibrates chamber to chamber
Within my heart,
A heart seated deep
Within the bosom of love
And ardent devotion?

Is it Thy voice
That captures my soul
And holds it fast
By chains and shackles
Of wonderment and amazement,

Chains and shackles
Softer than springtime showers,
More caressing than moonglow
On a summer night
Scented by
The sweet honeysuckle
Of enkindlement and fervor?

Or might it be
Chorus upon chorus
That I hear,
Each chorus chanted
By mystic damsels
In lavender-perfumed
Arabian melodies and Persian song,
Black-eyed beauties
The movement
Of whose luminous fingertips
Causes spiritual passion
To burn
And holy rapture
To blaze,
Mystic damsels,
The ruby redness of whose lips
Bestows blush to the cheeks
Of young maidens?

If this be true,
Were they created within
Supernal realms of glory
To delight eye and soul
Of splendorous,

Spiritual Luminaries
Whose twinkle of the eye
Births starry nights,
Spins off spiral galaxies,
Fuels the sun,
Blesses the dawn?

Or is that resounding,
Pervading voice
The voice of wonder and awe
From realities deep within,
Where Mystery, life and soul
Rendezvous, embrace,
And the soul,
Swooning away
And sailing on mystic breezes,
Surrenders
To heavenly gifts
From the Unseen?

Whatever the voice may be,
This I know:
Only from Thee,
Do rapture and wonderment,
Beauty and transcendence
Flow.

And for this,
Let the music play!
Let Thy Voice be heard!
Let my heart surrender
To the call of rapture and wonderment!
For my ears crave their beauty,

And my soul,
Adamant, unrelenting,
Refuses to relinquish
Its hearing!

Chariots of Fire

Chariots of fire,
Raised high by the flaming passion
Of the love of God,
Blazing luminosities of godliness and grace
Drawn by galloping steeds
Of boundless strength and undying benevolence
Riding upon mighty winds
And transforming gales of Revelation,
Race through time and space,
Traverse eternity,
Permeate ever-expanding realms of the spirit,
Set ablaze hearts in quest of the Beloved,
Souls searching, calling out,
For all that is holy,
Vitalizing and pure.

Chariots of fire,
Blazing torches of truth and testimony
Proclaiming the Unseen,
Their dauntless steeds propelled
By the breath of God,
He Who begets breath and flame,
Move through eastern skies
Of the heart,
Dawning place of spiritual awakening,
On celestial winds
As the eagle,
Lord and master of the heavens,
Fearless and without peer,

Proclaims majesty over flight and sky,
Soars the clear and stormy blue,
Rises high above mountaintops,
Conquers lofty summits,
Towering testimonials
To unyielding faith and faithfulness.

Chariots of fire,
Ineffably glorious,
Flaming realities of love and truth,
Set ablaze
Celestial realms and supernal skies,
Then rush forth at the speed of mystery
To illumine heart,
Thrill mind,
Infuse awe and wonderment,
Rapture,
Into the soul of creation,
That the ecstasy of love and joy of reunion
Permeate all that is,
Enkindle every good,
Excite every atom to testify
To the supreme singleness, might and majesty,
Of love and truth,
That they illumine the soul of humanity,
Dispel woe and ruin,
Conquer hate and disdain,
And awaken all peoples to the glorious purpose
For which they were created –
The organic unity,
Universal peace and prosperity
Of all mankind.

Come with Me!

Should you prefer the darkness,
I leave it to you!
It is yours!

Should your heart prefer the gloom,
This, too, I leave to you!
It holds no interest for me!

Should your soul prefer to bask
In benighted realms,
Shadowy climes
And obsidian abodes within,
Be assured,
These, too,
I leave to you,
For these are naught
But realms of despair!

But should you wish
To flee the darkness
And leave behind the dread of gloom,
Abandon stygian realms
That crush the spirit and stifle the soul,
Then come with me
To the splendorous, brilliant realms
Of the heart,
And illumined, sunlit skies
Of the soul,

Shining oceans of wisdom and joy
Surging deep within,
There to dance and play,
Love and learn,
In pulsating rays
Of miraculous,
Gleaming,
Spiritual Light!

Dance with Me!

While strolling the Avenue of Love
I heard an impassioned lover
Calling to his beloved.
His words, sweet to the ear,
I still recall:

Dance with me
On the stage of love
Far above the illusion of time,
Hand in hand, soul by soul,
In bosom-close, spiritual embrace,
Our heavenly steps choreographed
By unrehearsed affection
In gliding moves and supernal twirls
Of enduring trust and constancy.

Dance with me
As the gentle breezes of spring
Dance and waft through vale and garden,
Caressing every flower,
Romancing eager leaves
That rustle to the vernal rhythms
Of life renewed, revived,
Awakened.

Dance with me
To the unexplored depths
Of the ocean of love,
Where the seas of our affection

Meet and merge,
Where lustrous pearls of devotion
Gleam and shine,
And towering, cresting waves
Rise high in the heavens
In praise of the God of love,
Then rush to the awaiting shores
Of all that love can be.

Dance with me
In blooming gardens of delight,
Of purity and beauty
Planted by the hand of tenderness
And that, side by side,
Grow as one;
Where orange blossoms
On the tree of love
Perfume heart and soul
With timeless adoration
Wafted heart to heart;
Where hyacinth and jasmine
Beckon the sun,
And shining in the light of truth,
Call aloud to lovers;
Where warbling nightingales,
Intoxicated
By the Rose of Love,
Sing melodies too sweet to recall,
And enchanted lovers
Walk fragrant, rose-lined paths
Strewn with petals of joy and happiness.

Dance with me,
In the bright of day

And romantic still of night,
A dance of everlasting love
To dance across bursting dawns
Arrayed in red, orange and gold,
And breathtaking sunsets
That fill with wonder,
Warm the souls,
Of lovers young and old,
Greet the fall of night
And call to starry skies
And tales told only
By the whispering glow
Of moonlight.

Dance with me
Across the ages
And limitless expanse of love
In close embrace,
Eternally wed in pure devotion,
Undying fealty,
Our hearts and souls,
All that we are,
As one,
Fully alive to life and love,
The Eternal and eternity.

Dance with me
On the stage of love
Now and for all time,
For my heart can be for no other,
And it will never dance –
Can never dance! –
Unless it dance
With you!

Diana

*In remembrance of my dearly loved sister, Diana, who winged
her flight years ago to worlds beyond.*

In Paradise she dwells,
Silhouetted in white,
Clothed in prayer,
Draped in love,
Light,
Eternity –
Yet, I feel her near.

I call her name,
"Diana,"
Then gently whisper,
"Alláh-u-Abhá![1]
My dearly missed,
Beloved sister."

To this I hear her imagined reply,
"Alláh-u-Abhá!
Dear brother." –
Her greeting emerges
As sunlit vowels
And consonants
Clothed
In rainbows of affection –
These flourish
In the love
I bear her.

Tears fall,
Sweet memories of years past –
Indelible treasures
So dear since her passing –
Flush the heart's swelling,
Willing chambers,
Then rush through my soul,
Nourishing rivers of remembrance.

My soul calls aloud:
O, beloved sister!
Should it be His pleasure,
We will, together,
Rejoice
In the vast celestial realms
Of the hereafter,
Imbibe the sweet wine
Of reunion,
Bear witness to His Grace and Being,
Recount days gone by,
Then arise,
Servants to His Throne of Glory,
Irresistibly impelled
By Word and Revelation
To serve,
With countless others known and loved,
His Splendorous,
Mighty Cause of Oneness
In the Great Beyond.

---

[1] lit. God is Most Glorious; a greeting that Bahá'ís use when they meet each other.

Dream!

Dream
With throbbing imagination,
Pulsating certitude,
Undying conviction
Of all that awaits
A spiritually illumined,
Just and empowered
Humanity!

Dream,
Forever dream,
On uplifting,
Rose-scented breezes of passion
And zephyrs of zeal perfumed in parijat!

Dream
Of a New Day,
A Day raised high above
Thundering contention
And the dark, stormy clouds of strife
By mighty winds of pure,
All-embracing love!
If this be not our glorious future,
For what, then,
The struggle of the ages,
God-intoxicated lovers,
The dawn and rise
Of Truth,
Incandescent,

Traversing the long ecliptic
Of time?

Dream
With undimmed hope
And unrestrained fervor
Of hearts awakened to compassion,
Enkindled with love,
Illumined souls,
Who,
Like beams of caressing light
And glimmering waves of kindliness
Shine forth with glistening care
And glowing concern
For each and all!

Dream
In exuberant flows
Of jubilant hope
And rejoicing assurance
Of a new world,
A world at peace,
Organically one,
A world celebrating,
At long last and for all time,
All peoples, all cultures,
A world embracing
As firmly, as gently,
As a mother embraces her babe,
The full, rich
And even unexpected
Spectrum of human expression,
Contribution and diversity!

Dream,
Even as vernal, dancing winds –
Unafraid, determined,
Impatient to dance across
The stage of land and sea
And lingering earthly cares –
Dance to the impatient rhythms
Of ancient promise
And resonant melodic tones
Of irrepressible fulfillment
And destiny!

Dream
With fiery assurance
Of brightly lit tomorrows
For mother and child,
Father and son,
Rich and poor,
Tomorrows transformed
By gleaming rays
Of equity and contentment
For every soul,
Tomorrows bursting with splendor and awe,
Possibilities unimagined,
Tomorrows waiting,
Impatiently waiting,
For dreamers who make
Dreams come true!

Dream!
Imagine all that can be!
Fly your dreams
Across grand illumined skies!

Let them play and soar amidst
Translucent, welcoming love,
Wandering clouds of wonderment
And shining rainbows
Celebrating friendship and affection
In ethereal colors
Painted upon the mystic canvas
Of the sky of dreams
By the supernal brush
Of the Eternal,
He Who is Unknowable,
Unseen!

Dream!
Let us dream
With all our souls,
All that we are,
All we hope to be!
And then,
Let us act,
Free of doubt,
Assured, confident,
Even should it be for a lifetime,
For action is that magical elixir
That turns dreams,
Beautiful, brilliant dreams,
Into beautiful, brilliant,
Blissful tomorrows!

Drench My Soul

Drench my soul,
O Lord,
With the Wine
Of Thy Love.
Intoxication,
If it please Thee,
Be my fate.

Immersed
In the Sea
Of Thy Inebriation,
From each Pearl
I grow weary
Of this world.

Every Word,
O Beloved of my heart,
Each Verse,
O King of my soul,
These alone
Carry me away
To the Realms
Of rapturous stupor,
From which
I wish
Never
To return.

Give me to drink,
O Beloved of my heart,
All
That is with Thee.
This alone do I ask,
That forever in Thy Love
I may roam,
Throughout eternity,
I may bask.

Exquisite Illusion

Exquisite illusion,
Matter,
All that we see,
All that we touch,
That touches us,
Lest it be of the heart.

Exquisite illusion,
Time,
Empty space,
Creation from nothingness.

Exquisite illusion,
Wealth and fame,
Pride and worldly glory.

Exquisite illusion,
People of power, the powerful,
The god of self.

Exquisite illusion,
Life's journey on this pebble of a planet,
Lest it be of mind, heart and spirit –
Sojourners in this world but not of it!

Faithfulness

Faithfulness,
Prized beauty,
Damsel of the Divine,
To what sacred realms have you flown?
To what retreats of glory have you fled?
Have you abandoned us,
Left us to our own selves,
Or is it we that have abandoned you?
We miss the unfailing gifts you bring,
Long for the firm assurance of your gaze,
Your clear, unequivocal, unwavering voice,
The confirming wave of your steady hand!

Splendrous angel from on high,
Your beauteous visage we remember well,
We recall it often!
Your shining countenance –
Guiding light of fidelity and beacon of hope
That has shone across the ages –
Seems unknown, unwelcome, a stranger
To many a heart,
Benighted in many a soul!
Some have pushed you aside,
Held you low,
Scoffed at your beauty,
Then banished you to the cold, forsaken tomb
Of an unrepentant, wayward heart,
There to fade from memory,
Perish among the forgotten.

Faithfulness,
Watchful maiden,
How brightly you once lit city and town,
Hall and home, work and play!
How you shone in the hearts of lovers!
From time immemorial
Friend and stranger,
Kith and kin,
People rich and people poor,
Have been illumined
By your ineffable brilliance,
Dazzling hues of fidelity!
Regrettably,
There were always those
Who turned aside from your counsel,
But, alas,
Not like today!

Exalted damsel
Descended from realms above,
Your every breath and word,
Born of hallowed Spirit –
The Most Great Spirit –
Proclaim your timeless truths,
The unerring,
Never-beguiling lessons
You have to teach.
It is ours,
Each and every one,
To rendezvous with your essence,
Seek with diligence your sacred tryst,
Revel in the rapture of your presence!

Faithfulness,
Chaste and holy maiden,
Captivate our hearts!
Render us but thralls
Of your undeniable beauty!
Keep us near!
Clutch us to your bosom!
Treasure us
As we must, for the good of all,
Treasure you!

Shining damsel
Ordained by the Almighty,
I beseech you,
Stray not far,
For we,
Bereft of your light,
The bright rays of trust you engender,
Will stumble and fall,
Wander into the darkness
Of a black, forbidding,
Unholy night.

Faithfulness,
Beauteous maiden –
Your heavenly countenance,
Lovelier than the page can portray –
Let your resplendent visage shine!
Let the bell-like peals
Of your resonating voice be heard!
Desert us not!
Hold us close and closer still,
That the vitalizing warmth of your beating heart
Penetrate our souls,

Ignite a fire within our hearts and minds
That will blaze with your glorious light,
Set us aflame to seek all that you are,
All we are meant to be,
All we must become!

Fallen Leaves

Musings on a Wisconsin fall morning

Fallen leaves
Upon the ground,
Awaiting earth's full,
Inevitable embrace,
Tell us your tales,
Whispered
From passing winds
Caressing you tenderly
As though a new-born babe,
Or shaking you violently
As you held on to life,
And twig and branch.

I see you now
As I see myself,
Leaves yellowed
From time and destiny,
Though, unlike you,
I know not my fate,
Or what good
Given
To a fast-fleeting life.

When the fall of my life
Moves on
To the final winter
Of my years,
And the last leaves

Of my outward being
Are consigned,
Like yours,
To the cold,
Barren ground,
His Call will awaken me
And call me to account
For a life graciously bestowed.
Only then
Will my soul find rest,
Though it be consigned,
Like the fallen leaves
Of our outward being,
To a chill, barren tomb,
For His pleasure alone
Do I seek.

But should He
Beckon me to Life,
I will awaken to His Call,
Thankful, humbled,
And like you,
Rest
In the Garden
Of His Will,
And the Sanctuary
Of His Pleasure,
To rise once again
Amidst the Verdure
Of His Eternity,
And thrill
To the Whispering Winds
Of His Love.

Farewell, Sweet Maiden

For the day when the pen no longer moves and the page remains
forever bare

Farewell,
Sweet maiden –
Our rendezvous has been sweet,
Long-lived, enriching.

Your voice,
Music to my heart,
Rhythm to my soul,
Has thrilled me for so long
But, at long last,
It is time for us to part –
Lovers forever,
Adoring friends for all time.

I will miss your beauteous visage,
Your countenance fair,
Your smile born of allusion,
Depth and meaning,
Your kindness beyond compare.

Poetry,
Sweet maiden,
Be well,
Thrill your lovers
As only you can do
And,

Should you be so inclined,
Remember me,
As well,
If only
From time to time.

Fiery Flames and Bursting Rays of Love

Fiery flames
And bursting rays
Of love –
Sacred nectar of the divine –
May these fiercely burn,
Illumine
Heart and soul,
Mind and aspiration,
And reduce to ash
Untoward mountainous forests
Of doubt and disillusion,
Worldly passions and desires
Unworthy
Of God-given nobility.

And may
The scorching,
Seething flames
And ruinous, searing fires
Of an unsound and baneful character
Be fully extinguished
By the holy,
Inimitable revelations
Of His will and purpose,
And then,
A thing forgotten,
Be condemned eternally
To the graveyard
Of oblivion –

All that once was
But never again,
Will be.

Fire Lily

Fire lily,
African sleeping beauty
Deigning only to arise from smoke and ash,
What love, undeviating devotion,
Compels you to unfailingly awaken,
Arise from a long sleep and unknown dreams
That only you and Mother Nature know?

Why the abeyance
To show yourself,
Proclaim your beauty,
Admittedly modest though it may be,
Smile broadly your scarlet smile
And shine boldly forth in brilliant red
On torched and scarred land,
A testimony to hope and life,
A witness to rebirth and beauty,
Renewal, all that will thrive and flourish
Once again?

Fire lily,
It seems that the warm embrace of raging flame
And the torrid kiss of blazing fire
Are to you
As the vitalizing kiss
Of the first days of spring
And the benevolent, uplifting embrace
Of vernal zephyrs
Are to hyacinth and daffodil,

Milkweed and dandelion –
How soft that springtime kiss,
How tender, gently flowing,
Those zephyrs!
How far removed
From your fiery awakening!

Or might it be
That Mother Nature
Has betrothed you to the crown prince
Of vivifying, benevolent fire
Whose warm, loving lips –
And no other –
Can put bright red blush
To your patient, waiting cheeks?
I recall a storybook maiden
Who awakened the same!

Fire lily,
Your scarlet blooms,
Bowed down as in prayer,
Betoken a humility
Sorely lacking in the human world.
Would that we could learn this from you!
Too many the human flowers
Sorely in need of that godly quality!
So many the human hearts
Colored and stained in false pride and arrogance
That forever deny true beauty and charm,
Belie spiritual and natural attraction.

Lovely maiden,
Flower of the Cape,

Unassuming, resolute,
Determined to burst forth and bloom,
You call to mind Phoenix-like lovers
Who,
Godly, courageous, born anew,
Rise from the ash of lifeless,
Outworn doctrines that debilitate
And prejudices, cruel and unholy,
That dishonor and destroy.
Like you,
They stand in bold relief,
Brilliant against the ashen darkness
Of our times,
Unwilling to surrender
To a landscape charred, desolate.

Fire lily,
The mystery of your spectacular rise
Intrigues me,
Captivates my soul,
Your patience and long-suffering
Give pause to wonder,
To reflection on the life of the soul.
Your humility
And exquisite, timely poise,
Worthy of note,
Worthwhile to ponder,
Beckon unfoldment by the wise,
Compel questions
Of purpose and meaning.

African beauty,
Amazing, faithful and true,

May you
Forever rise from the ash
And bloom,
Adorned in red,
A flaming Phoenix born of fire
To proclaim,
Bear witness to,
Despite scorched, stark ground,
The power of undying faith
And unwavering faithfulness,
Rejuvenating hope,
And colorful,
Vibrant days to come,
With their sunlit morns
And fragrant,
Brilliant tomorrows.

Flight of Life

Flight of years
In heavens far-flung
And heavens close,
How quickly you pass,
Making your way on blowing gales
Of chance and destiny,
Gentle winds and softly flowing breezes
Of time and swiftly passing days.

Flight of time
You seem to wing your way
As birds fly,
Rising high on warm, upward flows
Of good fortune,
Then gliding,
Happily, effortlessly,
Through the quiet moments
Of our lives.
And then, at times,
It seems you burst forth,
A peregrine falcon,
Soaring to a great height
Then diving with dazzling speed
In quest of some prey.

Flight of life,
How you elude us so
With the passing of days and hours!
Do we truly believe

We will fly these mortal skies forever,
That the boughs and branches
Of the tree of our lives
Will ever welcome us
To their strong, outstretched arms,
And that the leaves
Of our words and deeds
Will rustle on this earthly plane
Without end,
Even as springtime zephyrs,
Year after year,
Faithfully return?

Flight of years,
With the passing of time
We will wing our flight
To the Great Beyond,
There to fly skies
Of our own making,
Be they high or low,
Sunlit or cloudy.

But should it be His pleasure,
His ever-abounding grace
Will surround us and lift us high
That we may see, with clear vision,
The flight of our years
In the skies or our lives
Through His eyes –
Eyes of grace and mercy,
Compassion and forgiveness,
Eyes that see our souls
Soaring mystic heights

In the boundless firmament
And everlasting heavens
Of His glorious,
Infinite,
All-embracing love.

Friendship, My Old Friend

Friendship,
My old friend,
How pure your motive,
Sincere your intent,
Unwavering your constancy!
You are even as the zephyrs of spring
To the shy, poetic daffodil,
Drenching rains to thirsty,
Dry ground.

From time immemorial,
Like the gentle bursting of dawn,
You have warmed heart and home,
Illumined thought and mind.
You have walked every land
As clouds traverse the heavens,
Danced every song
As blossoms dance the wind.

Your feats border the miraculous.
Truly,
You are a heavenly seed that gives flower
To kindliness and goodness, generosity and love,
For you have succored the poor,
Counseled the rich,
Uplifted the downtrodden,
Revitalized the despairing and despondent.
As certain as the rising of the moon
And its steady climb,

You have encouraged budding lovers,
Built ties too deep, too strong to be broken.

Sadness and joy,
Too,
Know you well,
As do battlefield and calm,
Ease and pain,
Playground laughter!
It seems you forever walk
Fields of flowers and fields of grain,
Endless avenues of endless towns,
The unpaved walkways
Of remote villages and distant haunts.

Friendship,
True and lasting,
Stand strong!
Hold your ground!
Beware,
Lest you go the way of the weak
And unprincipled,
Those who feign friendship
For personal gain.
Yours is to take our hand,
Ease the way
Through the darkness of our times
By the lights of constancy and caring,
Beams of thoughtfulness and love,
Rays of sacrifice!

My old friend,
May all peoples honor you,

Walk with you!
For it is yours
To remain firm and fast
In all that you practice and teach.
And when last days fall
And the sun sets on the horizon
Of our lives,
May we reflect the light
Of your illumined countenance,
See but the good in one another,
Be understanding and giving to the end,
Stay true to your example.

Friendship,
Be well, live long!
May you forever bring,
As surely as the wind blows
And summer follows spring,
Solace and strength,
Courage and integrity
To all who know you,
Each and every one,
And without exception!

Friendship

*In honor of two dear souls and an angel who has winged her
flight*

What words have we
When His grace falls as rain,
And love finds souls
Whose hearts soar
On lofty gales and spiritual winds?

Words of praise and no other!
Comes the reply,
For all else crawls upon the ground,
Besmirched and tattered,
Unworthy of mention.

Still, for He has said it so,
Words of friendship
He loves to hear,
And for this,
I pen these humble lines!

From the Eye of the Beloved

From supernal heights of glory
Where benevolence and holiness,
Creativity and grace
Come forth to renew and replenish
All that is,
A teardrop of love and joy
From the eye of the Beloved
Descended
In mighty crescendos of Revelation,
Power and Light
To water all creation,
Infuse new life
Into worlds seen and unseen,
Revive
Movement and stillness,
Ethereal causalities.

With that tear
Expressions of truth,
Vitalizing, hidden, unimagined,
Sprang forth
In the hearts of the faithful.
Anemones of spiritual light
Flourished in the souls of lovers.
Roses full, ruby red and white,
Betokening sacrifice and selflessness,
Bloomed in hearts pure.
Nightingales,
Warbling love songs from realms above –

Intoxicated lovers, songsters of truth –
Circled those sacred blooms
With reverence and awe.
And in the hearts of the righteous,
Jasmine and hyacinth flowered
To perfume ardent souls
In quest
Of the Divine Beloved.

From the Visage of the Beloved
Came forth a smile,
For His tear had fallen true,
Releasing oceans of surging beneficence
And seas of billowing bounty.
The heavens were renewed
And the flame of the spirit,
Enkindled by the love of God,
Blazed forth,
Incandescent,
Across eastern and western skies,
And worlds of holiness
Beyond the shackles of matter,
Space and time.

From that tear of love and joy
The New Day came forth.
The Sun of Truth dawned anew
Then rose high
To shine in splendor
From the apex of promise.
The nighttime of past ages fell,
Never to rise,
And the Moon of Mystery

Shone,
Aglow in brilliant servitude,
Illuminating the Straight Path –
Eternal,
Inviolable avenue guiding lovers
To the garden of the heart,
Quiescence,
Illumination of the soul,
Murmuring brooks and gently flowing streams
Of sacred law and radiant realities
Moving deep within.

Such is verse
Penned in praise of the Beloved
With the ink of the heart
From this poet's feeble hand,
Verse awaiting
Some heart to ponder,
Some soul to muse,
Some kindly eye to read,
These humble,
Simple lines.

From the Rose Garden

From the rose garden,
Sweet savors of holiness
Wafting from the Rose of Love.

From the rose garden,
Redolence to perfume humanity,
All peoples, all kindreds.

From the rose garden,
Fragrance so pure, so sublime
As to enthrall the souls of lovers,
Enrapture hearts seeking, longing, waiting,
Enchant the soul of mankind.

From the rose garden,
Softly flowing winds of unity,
Fast-flowing zephyrs of compassion,
Transcendence.

From the rose garden,
Abounding and abiding love,
Peace and composure.

From the rose garden,
The mystical call to enter,
Abide therein, rendezvous
With the rapturous
Rose of Love.

Giving Hands

Giving hands,
Though cupboards be nigh bare –
Hands truly giving!

Selfless, tender care,
Though ingratitude the reward –
Care truly selfless, tender!

Kindly words,
Though vitriol be returned –
Words truly kind!

Trustworthy friends,
Unswerving, no matter cost or price –
Friends truly trustworthy!

Understanding hearts,
Free of judgment, replete of wisdom –
Hearts truly understanding!

Truthful souls,
These speak to truth undeterred by opprobrium –
Souls truly truthful!

Illumined, thoughtful minds,
Bright amidst the darkness –
Minds truly illumined, thoughtful!

Lovers of humanity,
Proclaiming diversity, oneness, cooperation –
Souls truly lovers!

Loving countenances,
Though contempt, alone, be returned –
Countenances truly loving!

Undaunted seekers,
Unafraid, questing after meaning, truth –
Seekers truly undaunted!

Patient multitudes,
Though scorned and poor –
Multitudes truly patient!

Unrelenting resolve and strength,
Though face-to-face with the menacing stare of prejudice –
Resolve and strength truly unrelenting!

Unwavering faith,
Though the struggle be hard –
Faith truly unwavering!

These
Are godly and to be praised,
Earth's treasures,
A blessing to all –
Of these,
Truly,
The world needs more!

Goddess of Verse and Rhyme

Enchanting beauty,
Dance with me!
Open wide your enthralling arms
That I might enter the bosom
Of your alluring embrace.

Winsome damsel
Draped in syllable and sound,
Wrapped in thrilling rhyme
And adorned with tales
Of ancient lore,
Sweep me away to heavenly realms
Where angels play,
And moonlight and magic,
Betrothed,
Dance across the spheres as one
On scrolls of inspiration.

Enticing beauty,
Clothed in swirling crescendos
And choreographed truths,
Your strutted stretches and strides
Across the stage of wonderment
Stir my imagination,
Plunge deep my soul
In oceans of reflection!

Maiden fair,
Pray tell your name,

Lest the rapture of its melodic beauty,
The sensuousness of its sound,
Denied me,
Haunt my days.
Softly, sweetly,
More delicate than springtime blooms,
More gentle than a lover's touch,
Comes the reply:

Poetry,
Goddess of Verse and Rhyme,
Is my name,
A name bestowed in ancient times.
If enamored of my beauty
And impassioned
To dance my depths,
If your heart be strong
And swift your feet,
Your soul unfettered
And eager to fly,
Then, come!
Dance with me!

Heavenwards

Heavenwards,
That is where
The bird of my heart
Longs to fly,
Where larks sing
And angels play melodies
On the wind.

Heavenwards,
Up, up,
And higher still,
Where peace abounds
And the sky is blue,
Where the sun is bright
And clouds play
And reminisce.

Heavenwards,
Where hearts are pure
And words are sweet,
Where love surrounds
And friends gather,
As one,
No matter
Where they be!

I Heard a Poet Say

I heard a poet say
As he was musing with the wind,
Taking into account
The simple, inconsequential gifts
He had to offer:

It is not mine,
Nor will it ever be,
To build bridges to span the waters,
That,
Like majestic,
Grand Sequoias or the Grand Teton
Stand strong and tall.
Such accomplishments are for a gifted few.
The share of this soul
Is but a simple heart, a weak hand
To move the pen
In hopes of words to traverse
Mystic seas of wonder
That rise and surge within
And pay homage to
The quiet, pondering shores
Of the soul.

It is not mine to heal the sick,
Make them whole,
Prolong life for even a day.
Such a gift
God has bestowed on others.

Nonetheless,
I hear the call of pen and page
And strive,
Despite faltering attempts,
To give solace to the heart
Burdened by the vicissitudes
That weigh it down.
Though a healer I will never be,
Still,
I search for words
Of balm and comfort
To uplift the spirit,
Bring relief to the soul,
Show the way to seekers
Whose hearts ache for truth,
Yearn for tranquility and peace.
If not for this,
For what, then,
Poetry?

I have not such brilliance
As to raise towering monuments
And architectural feats
That proclaim grandiosity
To sky and cloud,
Flocking birds and rising moons.
No such mind have I,
Though, truly,
I marvel
At such lofty accomplishments,
For at best,
I can write but verse and line
That struggle to lift, raise high,

Meaning and rhyme
That perhaps,
If the pen be kind
And the ink willing,
Humble edifices of poetic,
Cogent thought
Be raised
In the city of the heart
And take their rightful place
On the grand avenues of the soul.
But, alas,
And this I know,
For me
This may never be!

Great seagoing vessels
And those that plunge the deep,
These never will I conceive nor fashion.
Such complexity
My mind can neither fathom nor grasp.
How thankful I am for those that can!
But line by line
And unafraid of what lies below,
I try to plunge
The surging seas within,
Dive their depths
For pearls of shining profundity
Held close and dear
In timeless shells of ancient beauty.
And if this I can do,
I will rise
To ride grand, rushing waves,
Heaving walls of truth and wonder

That hold aloft tales of yore
And proclaim with surging power
The oneness
Of the great sea of life.

Such is the plight of a humble poet
Whose gifts are few.
But, alas,
It is not mine to ask for more,
Nor could I ever wish
For aught else.

I Saw a Drop

I saw a drop
Rise up,
Challenge
The sea,
Fall to great depths
Of ingratitude
And ingratiation,
A mere wisp
Seemingly daring
All creation,
Playing to the caprices
Of the evanescent.

I saw it boldly,
Vacuously,
Testify
To its life-giving waters,
Then dry up
On hot, deserted,
Wind-blown sands
Of self-love –
No audience applauded
Its vile arrogance.

I saw the Ocean
Reach out
And lift it up
In tender solicitude

And give it life
And form
And draw it back
Unto itself
And hold it close
And dear –
No words of rebuke
Did I hear,
No frowns of scorn
Could I see.

It was then
That I saw the face
Of forgiveness –
It was then that I saw
The face of God.
It was then
That I witnessed
Grace,
All-encompassing –
And encompassing
All mankind.

I Take the Pen

A flirtation with rhyme

I take the pen
In hopes
That words of praise
Ascend,
And lines of love,
Worthy, unafraid,
Fly high.

Yet they wander aimlessly,
Forever without wing,
Strangers to lofty blowing winds
And grand, roaming clouds,
Unsung guardians of the heavens,
Unchallenged masters of the sky!

O that my pen would learn
Lessons of love
My heart has tried to teach,
That a word or two or even more,
Be as falcons of love to the page,
Majestic eagles of word and rhyme,
That to lofty heavens reach!

Again,
The pen
I take in hand,
The nib I put to page,

Then write from heart and soul
And realms within,
Lines of love that strive to rise,
Give flight to reflection and pause,
In hopes they soar in praise of Him
And heart and mind bow low,
Eager to engage!

Soon the ink
No longer flows,
Clamoring to be dry.
Hearing this,
My words, despondent and forlorn,
Make home the lowly ground,
And frightened of lifting winds and sky,
Are too cowardly to venture forth,
Too afraid to even try!

The lines I pen,
Would that they could soar and fly!
But bereft of sonorous wind
And eloquent wings for lyrical flight,
They flee from wind and zephyr,
For these can lift them high!

They choose instead to make their way
Upon a cold and lonely path.
Hidden in the darkness,
Unknown, unseen,
It is there they make their home,
Free from derision,
Unwarranted but expected wrath!

It is then I hear
From pen and ink,
And even from the page,
Tears that fall as winter rain
From clouds that have no end,
Each a plea to still the pen,
That verse and prose I write no more,
That word and rhyme,
Like music poorly played,
No longer ear and eye offend!

Still,
There is hope.
All is not lost,
For the poetry of love
Is written clearly
On the pages of my soul,
And words of praise
Have long been inscribed,
Eloquent and true,
Upon the parchment
Of my heart.

For what purpose then,
Pen and ink,
Lines of love and praise,
Clever words and thoughtful rhyme
That fly across the ages,
Soar the untold ravages of time!

For verses,
Songbirds of my soul,
Warblers of my heart,

Have long been penned
In the mystic depths within,
There to nest and fly,
With no intention,
Ever, to depart!

If I stumble

If I pass you by
With sorrow as my guide,
Please take my hand,
Lead me to a better place.

If I stumble and fall,
Unable to find my balance,
Please lift me up –
The ground of uncertainty
Is cold and damp.

If I fail to do my part,
Please show me how,
Truly, I wish to learn.

If I seem invisible,
As I often do,
Please see me
So I know I exist.

If you can find it in your heart
To look deep within my soul
And find some long-lost good,
Then, truly,
With hope renewed,
My humanity confirmed,
I will turn to life,

Arise,
And take up,
Once again,
The struggle.

If Sail You Must

Love,
Sail not away
From the harbor of my heart,
Lest the sun of my soul forever set
And the moon of my being cease to rise.

Rather,
Let all that is not of thee sail away
Into the dark horizon of unbelief and pride,
There to gasp and die, fade away,
Even as the dark of night
Before an emerging,
Brilliant dawn.

And,
If sail you must,
Let us sail as one
Across the billowing seas of the soul
To mystic lands
And unsuspected islands of mystery
Where wind and gale,
Gulls of stunning wisdom and sanctity
Proclaim holiness,
Where fruits of the spirit
Are succulent and sweet,
And godliness,
Queen of attributes,
Waits patiently,
There to greet us,
Welcome us ashore.

If You Must

Travel east and west
If you must,
In search of truth and meaning,
Mystic knowledge and ancient tales,
Wonderment and all the gifts
That life can give.

Travel north and south,
If you will,
In search of all that soothes the heart
And satisfies the soul,
That releases the refreshing, cooling waters
Of contentment and happiness.

But should you dare,
And courage be your lot,
Dive deep within the mystic seas
Of soul and heart
To find peace, strength, tranquility,
All that you desire, aspire to,
For therein lies every joy,
Meaning unalloyed,
Beauty and transcendence,
All you seek.

In the Garden

A reflection on the garden of life

In the garden –
Nature's garden –
Cherry blossoms
To delight eye and heart,
Timeless beauty penned
In pink and white;

Plum blossoms
Wafting fragrance
To awaken the soul,
Perfume the dawn,
Call to blowing winds,
Tease land and rain;

Songbirds
Perched atop
The tree of tranquility
Trilling sweet arias,
Warbling songs of peace
And contentment;

Roses,
Ruby red and sunlit yellow,
Quiet pink and winsome white,
Queenly beauties
Enthroned on the seat of redolence,

Nightingales their most loyal,
Faithful subjects;
Butterflies,
Fluttering ballerinas
Playfully dancing flower to flower,
Each one adorned in color,
Dressed in light,
Their performance well-pleasing
To the eye of Nature;

All these
Reside in Nature's garden,
Yet remain wholly unaware
O the gardener
Who tends it.

In another garden –
The garden of our lives –
Souls giving and pure,
Who,
Even as cherry blossoms of spirituality,
Open and flower
On the outstretched branches
Of kindliness and love,
Then quietly dance through the air
On winds of grace and beauty
To gently touch, flow through,
The lives of others;

Souls tender and caring,
Fragrant plum blossoms of the spirit
That shine brightly,
Waft redolent hope

And fragrant encouragement
To sweeten the lives of young and old,
Lift high each and every drooping heart,
Saddened soul;

Individuals who,
Like songbirds of the heart,
Trill notes of abiding love
And lasting tranquility,
Warble tales of promise and affection,
Brilliant tomorrows,
Sing melodies of peace and promise
From lofty branches of equality,
Oneness;

In this garden
We find souls,
Flowering roses of renunciation
And selflessness
Eager to perfume passersby
And those who stop to linger
With attar of abiding love,
Roses of loving kindness
Whose fragrant, unfolding petals
Are as kindly smiles of mirth and warmth
On the coldest of life's
Winter days;

Butterflies
Of boundless grace,
Too,
Reside in this garden,
Virtuosos of virtue and goodness

That flutter and fly,
Heart to heart,
On zephyrs of sincerity and generosity
And softly blowing winds of fidelity
And faithfulness –

We all abide,
Make our home,
In this garden –
The garden of our earthly existence –
Is it not ours,
Then,
We who are endowed
With reason and understanding,
Unlike Mother Nature's
Flowering blooms and birds of song,
To ask of the gardener,
His nature and existence?

And if not
The Divine Gardener,
Who, then,
Planted the first seed?
Who, then,
Gave it life?

Inebriation

Of the Love of God

Intoxication,
Unseal your casks!
My thirst bears not
An empty glass!

Inebriation,
Seize my soul!
Your Wine
My being
Has redefined.

Red,
Deep red
Ruby Wine,
Relent not
Your hold on me.
Your madness has made
My spirit light
And,
Like a bird,
To His abode alone
I take my flight!

Inexorable!

The immutability of time,
The vastness of space,
Inexorable!

The rhythmic pulsations of life,
Birth and death,
Inexorable!

The unfailing blooming of spring,
Fruits of summer,
Inexorable!

The redolence of the rose,
The warbling of the nightingale,
Inexorable!

Plunging roots, tall and mighty trees,
Billowing oceans,
Surging seas,
Inexorable!

The setting of the sun,
The rising of the moon,
Brilliant orbs traversing nighttime skies,
Inexorable!

Good triumphing over evil,
Love over hate,

Peace over war,
Inexorable!

The clarion call of justice and fairness,
Equity and equality,
Freedom from oppression,
Inexorable!

The indomitable power of hope and promise,
Resilience and persistence,
Faith and fortitude,
Inexorable!

The slow, long, painful slog of human evolution,
Rise and fall,
Chaos and order,
Inexorable!

One human family,
Enlightened, unified,
Prosperous, creative, diverse,
Its realization assured,
Irresistibly unfolding across the near and distant reaches of time,
Inexorable!
Unequivocally inexorable!

It Is Love that Binds Us Together

I see your color,
You see mine.
It is love
That binds us together.

I know your heart,
You know mine.
It is love
That binds us together.

I trust your goodness,
You trust mine.
It is love
That binds us together.

I feel your pain,
You feel mine.
It is love
That binds us together.

From love,
All good, oneness are born.
In its absence,
There is only
Estrangement.

Justice, Where Have You Fled?

*Inspired by an evening with friends who have suffered the
indignities and pain of racial prejudice*

Justice,
You bring me joy,
Albeit seldom you visit!
Where is it that you have fled?
Your absence causes sorrows deep,
Brings pain, tears overflowing.

Justice,
You bring me joy!
Though your voice,
Seldom heard raised for the oppressed,
The suffering, the forgotten,
Is missed –
O so terribly missed!

Justice,
Hear our call!
Raise high your voice for all peoples,
All colors, in all climes,
For without you,
The pain
Is too much to bear,
Tranquility
Stands beyond reach,
And the lamentations of hearts
Too loud to quiet.

Liberty

Liberty,
Raise high your voice
For all to hear,
For the Beloved
Has set you free
From the dross
And malice
Of our times.

Your cage,
Now barren,
Is a glaring reminder
Of the darkness
That fastened your shackles
And locked your stocks.

Emerge,
O Beauty
Of Paradise prophesied.
Ring out
Peals of freedom,
Cries that raise
The oppressed.

Liberty,
Your sensuous beauty,
Now fully unveiled
To land and sea,
Soul and heart,

Beckons
An awaiting humanity
To liberty unknown,
Now glimpsed,
Soon to be
Unfolded.

Light

Light,
How I love the way
You dance
In crystal and gem,
On bright, green leaves,
Cherry blossoms and roses red,
Swaying trees and rushing streams,
On pond and brook,
And all that moves!
Would that
You would dance that way
In me!

I love the beauty
You reveal,
The warmth
You bestow!
I love the way
You charm the dawn,
Romance the setting sun,
Bathe young lovers
In your waves!

I love the way
You fill the day,
Charm the night,
Shine
In starlight and moonbeam,
Alike!

I love the way you glisten
On ocean waves
And snow-capped peaks!
Would that
You would shine so bright
In me!

I love the way
You give wing
To color and form.
How they thrill the eye!
I love the way
Butterfly wings bring joy
In the light of morn
And height of day!

Light,
I love all that you are,
Every word you say!
But should you be able,
Might I, too,
Imperfect though I be,
Shine bright,
Fully Illumined, warm of heart,
A torch or candle,
In the dark of day!

Lighthearted Humor Meets Sober Thought

Two men,
Long known to each other,
Engaged in an unexpected
But open and telling conversation
That follows:

The first man,
Well read, enlightened
And of good and generous heart,
Commented to the other:
"It seems in you
I see no highs or lows,
No joys, generosity of spirit,
Only denial of challenge
And throes."

The second man,
Gleefully glib, replied:
"What you say is true!
It is the latest rage,
The current fad,
Trend of the day!
They call it
'Bubble wrap of the soul.'"

The first man,
Amazed, left nigh speechless
By this comment,
Made the following observation:

"In you I see no passion for meaning,
No interest in the deeper,
Spiritual aspects of life,
No curiosity, zest for understanding,
Interest in the world
Or those around you."

The second man,
Eager to reply, said:
"Most assuredly, this is true!
It is the latest rage,
The current fad,
Trend of the day!
They call it
'Bubble wrap of the mind.'"

The first man,
Almost in unbelief
Of what he had heard,
Asked the other man:
"Why?
Why subscribe to such fads,
Trends of the day?"

The second man,
Clearly,
Thoroughly committed
And satisfied with
His trendy,
Fad-driven life, replied:
"They are the latest rage,
The current fads,
The trends of the day!

They call it
'Bubble wrap of mind and heart,
Soul and imagination.'"

Then he added,
Smugly but politely,
Assured in his conviction,
Confident in his own position:
"It is not for everyone,
Only the select, smart few!
Not those who think for themselves,
Feel, love and imagine,
Not for people like you!"

Many long year later
The two men met again,
Each pursuing life as before.
The first wore a smile,
The second wore a frown,
The first a testimony
To a life well lived,
The second a testimony
To a sad, disillusioned,
Regretful,
Motley clown!

Little Bird

Little bird,
Fluttering about branch to branch,
How I love to watch your wings
And wonder what they say.

Is every flutter a letter or word,
Timeless poetry that you fly,
Or are you writing tales of yore,
A manuscript, perhaps,
On the flight of birds,
Great and small?

And if verse you write,
Who, then,
Takes it to heart,
Muses on each line,
Grasps its import,
Recites its wisdom?
And if not bird or sky or blowing wind,
Is it, then, God alone,
For whom your write?
Or it it He
That has taught you verse,
Given you ink and pen?

And if for God, alone,
How can we read every line,
Or, maybe,
Just one or two?

How can we decipher
Your ancient, fluttering script,
The meanings,
Deep and profound,
Your proclaim
With every flap of wing?

The little bird,
Hearing the musings
Of my heart,
Came close,
And,
With the movement of its wings,
Whispered in my ear,
"The poetic verse, the sacred script,
The story I write
Is this –

Let your heart and soul
Fly high and higher still,
Far above
Cloud and hilltop
Of the worldly and mundane,
Where the air is pure
And words are kind,
Where love prevails,
And melodies of the spirit,
Ringing loud and true,
Can be heard,
And the poetry
Of the longing lover
In quest of the Beloved
Resounds across the heavens,

And the cry of the Beloved
Rings out,
'Here am I,
O seeker in quest of God!
Here am I,
O lover of truth!'"

Little Sparrow

Little Sparrow –
Flitting about
A gilded cage
Of pebbles and stone,
And memories
Unrepentant
And unrequited,
Of lights fluorescent
Where sun shines not,
And moonglow
Declines to enter
Amidst the dark songs
Of drifting values
Sadly sung –
Arise!

Ascend
Phoenix-like!
Eagle-like!
To the heavens
And where Destiny
Awaits you,
Anxiously,
With wings
And heart
And songs
Anew.

Little sparrow,
Exit your cage
And fly above the clouds
To Life,
To Joy,
To the Life-Giver!

It is He
Who will breathe into you
Songs Celeste
And point your way
To Paradise!

Lonely Raindrop

Lonely raindrop
Upon my window,
I see you forlorn,
Alone,
Trembling in the cold,
A fallen tear
Upon the ground,
Afraid, apprehensive,
Of what awaits you.

I watch the warmth
Of Mother Earth
Embrace you,
Wipe away your tear,
Turn it to joy
As it joins you as one
With drops you knew,
Danced with in skies above,
Missed terribly.

Now, joyous, alive with purpose,
You release yourself completely,
Sacrificially,
To water, become one with,
All living things.

Drop of rain,
Transformed, fully alive,
We have much to learn from you,

Lest tears of sorrow be our lot,
And loneliness
Our final abode.

Look Into My Eyes

Look into my eyes
And I will look into yours,
That we see naught but light
In each other.

Look into my heart
And I will look into yours,
That we see naught but good
In each other.

Look into my soul
And I will look into yours,
That we see naught but beauty
In each other.

Look into me
And I will look into you,
That we see naught but hidden treasures
Of mind and heart and soul
Deep within,
Eager to be seen and explored,
Discovered and embraced,
For goodness abounds
And we have but to open
Eye and mind and heart
To see it!

Love and Verse

The poet sets free
Love and verse upon the page.
Unrestrained,
They prance and play,
Ride high the limpid blue waters
And billowing, silver-tipped waves
That thrust hard and long,
Crest high and higher still
To implore sun and sky
For inspiration.
Unabashed, unashamed,
These rise, come forth
From unrelenting gales
And blowing winds
Of the poet's imagination.

They then plunge,
Wide-eyed, determined, unafraid,
The mystic depths
Of quietude and contemplation
To explore gleaming, lustrous pearls
Of truths long treasured,
Nurtured, protected by,
Ancient, sheltering shells
Of profundity,
Of infinite, unbounded wisdom.

Arising from those depths
And eager to fly,

They soar supernal realms
Upon mighty gusts of wonderment
High in the ethereal heavens
Of spiritual revelations
Calling, beseeching, awaiting
To be unfolded.
Their flight complete,
They search out the garden of the heart,
Therein to ponder eternal questions
Beside still, sunlit ponds
Of unveiled purpose and intention,
Murmuring brooks
Of mortality and the immortal.

Released
To romp and roam
At will,
They seek to unfold concealed realities
From veiled mysteries
Folded deep into the soil of creation.
These,
Ready, hoping to be brought forth,
Beseech Nature to bloom, flower,
Take root,
Flourish upon the page.

Not content with such frolicking,
Love and verse seek out
Trilling songbirds of the spirit
To capture enrapturing, ancient melodies
Destined to be transcribed upon the page.
Still wanting more,
They call to the winds

For enlightenment,
Then look to the butterfly and rose
For gentleness and beauty,
That these
Touch and grace the page,
Temper the pen,
Console the struggling poet
In his endless quest.

Hearing the call to beauty,
They vibrate to harmonies
Born of night
And melodies that shine
With the rising of the dawn,
That emerge from raging falls
And quiet meadows,
The flapping of wings
And thunderous storms.
These they orchestrate
In notes of hope and light
To be played upon the page
In crescendos
Of rhythm and rhyme –
The poet's pen,
All the while helpless, submissive,
Moves only at their unyielding,
Adamant command.

The poet sets free
Love and verse upon the page,
Heart and mind
With but one intent,
That they be held close and dear

In the bosom of joy and love,
Thoughtfulness and understanding,
And that there,
Free and unrestrained,
They flourish,
Dance and play
Upon the endless lines
And untold pages
Of the reader's
Soul, mind and heart.

Love, Glorious Gift of the Eternal

War,
Never won,
At best, survived.

Hate,
Damned prescription
For death and misery,
Not life.

Love,
Glorious gift of the Eternal
To shine brightly from heart and soul,
To make as naught
The meandering dark shadows of self,
Avarice and pride,
And give brilliant, streaming
Light and life
To peace, tranquility, justice
For all mankind.

Love, Is That You I See?

Love,
Is that you I see
In blooming rose,
Queenly hyacinth,
Redolent blossoms of cherry,
Flowering plum?

Is that you I see
In cloud and wind and blowing rain,
Blankets of winter snow,
Proud rivers pulsating with life,
Diving mountain streams
And crashing falls
Unafraid of heights,
Meandering brooks
Whispering tales of love,
Quiet ponds
Reflecting purity of heart,
Gushing fountains
Proclaiming beauty of the soul?

Is that you I see
In hill and vale and mountain top,
Forests staunch and green,
In towering trees,
Their outstretched branches
Beseeching all that is holy, the benevolence of heaven,
Their roots strong and firm,
Immovable testimony to life and truth?

Is that you I see
In sun-drenched beaches,
Their sands inviting, sparkling white,
Love-struck waves rising high to glimpse
Waiting, adoring shores,
Red coral and pearls
From giving and mighty seas?

Is that you I see
In eagles high and nesting doves,
Summer winds and daffodils of spring,
Kindly faces and crying babes in mothers' arms,
Smiles of the good and caring,
Actions of the just and fair,
Furtive glances of lovers?

Love,
Is that you I see
In each and every thing,
At the stirring of dawn,
The mystic quiet of twilight,
The rising of the moon,
Shining of the sun?

Love,
It must be so,
For none dare challenge your claim,
Occupy your throne,
The seat whereon you reign,
Scepter in hand,
Ineffable in your beauty,
Boundless in your grace,
With none,
Past or present,
To rival you!

Lovely Daffodil

Lovely daffodil,
I see you smiling,
No longer sleeping
Beneath Nature's blankets
Of frost and cold
Or wishing for spring.

I see you playing
Ever so gently
In the breeze,
As a child at play,
Frolicking about
With joy,
Free of care.

Lovely daffodil,
Spring, at last,
Has sprung,
And you,
Dancing, floral ballerina
In green and gold,
Say it ever so sweetly
In your long-awaited,
Rising,
Delicate beauty.

Maiden Pure and True

Love,
Maiden pure and true,
May my every breath,
Even as a sweetly scented, salubrious wind,
Waft softly from the redolent rose gardens
Of thy presence
And fragrant fields of thy beauty
To move through and stir the lives of others,
Even as springtime zephyrs
Stir the morn.

May my pulsating, beating heart,
No longer mine but thine,
Pulsate and throb in complete surrender
To thy pleasure,
Its flowing crimson streams moving at thy will
In hopes of serving thee,
Attaining thine acceptance.

Beauteous maiden,
May my every wish be born of thee,
Alive to thy command,
A humble vassal and faithful servant
To thine unfading beauty,
Sublime countenance.

Love,
Effulgent maiden
Descended from the King of Glory,

May my eyes be illumined
By the dazzling rays
Beaming from the orb of thy beauty,
That I behold thee shining
In each and every soul,
A witness
To the lustrous gifts and talents
Of all peoples,
Their God-given beauty
And sparkling, precious gems of the spirit
Reflecting thy light.

And may my eyes,
Godly maiden,
Refuse the wanton darkness
And shadowy, lurking deceptions
Of seeing aught else but thee and thy purpose
In all created things,
Whether songbird or beetle,
Rose or thorn.

Love,
Maiden divine,
May my ears long for, hearken to,
Only thy sweet melodies,
The orchestral compositions of the heart
You pen,
The songs you sing,
The sacred hymns of the spirit
You compose and play
On the harp of timeless affection
And lute of eternal felicity,
Abiding tenderness.

Love,
Ethereal beauty,
Pure and true,
Walk with me,
Take my longing hand in yours,
Your luminous fingers intertwined with mine,
That they be as one.
Lead me, step by step,
To thy flowering gardens of spirituality,
Thy rushing streams and purling brooks
Of kindliness and compassion,
The heavenly,
Supernal realms of oneness, beauty,
Godliness.

May my soul,
O sweet maiden,
Humble and beseeching,
Pleading before thee,
Find neither rest nor repose
Except in thee,
My heart neither calm nor peace
Except in adoration
Of thine immortal perfections,
Immutable benevolence.

May my every hour pass,
O handmaiden of God,
In remembrance of thee,
My life be thine and thine alone,
For all else but thee is as naught,
Even as blowing sands
And passing winds,

A life ill-spent,
Forgotten,
Never lived.

Love,
Queenly maiden,
Purify my heart, transform me,
Enthrall all that I am and yearn to be
With your flaming fire that burns to ash
All that is not of thee,
All that is wholly unworthy of thy court,
That I may honor thee,
Prove my unwavering fealty
And undying devotion
Before thy throne.

O illustrious maiden,
Inspire the profound of my being
To embrace thee as no other,
Hold thee close
As the dawn holds the sun
And the heavens hold the night,
Clutch thee to my bosom as the blossoms of spring
Cling tightly to the branch, hold fast and firm
In coursing winds and drenching rain.

Love,
Beloved maiden,
Though my heart
Be far removed from thee
And my soul
Remote from thy presence,
Yet,

I long for thee to dwell within me,
Illumine my inmost essence,
Captivate my soul,
Resuscitate and recreate me,
For, alas,
Short of this,
My passing days
Are but a cold blowing wind
Meandering aimlessly
Across the seasons of my life;
Fallen leaves
And barren branches of the heart
Never to flower;
The bleak, harsh winter of my soul's end;
Verdant, blooming springs forever lost;
Summer fruits never ripened,
A life unfulfilled,
An end too burdensome,
Too heavy,
To bear.

Melodies of the Nightingale

Nightingale,
Warble your melodies,
Thrill our hearts with wonder,
Enchant our souls,
Cause our inmost realities
To fly high above space and time
To supernal realms of the spirit
In the lofty, mystic skies
Of sanctity and transcendence
Where faith reigns supreme
And the quest for the Beloved
Is the heart's only desire.

Nightingale
Perched high
In the tree of rapture,
Poised in tranquility
Upon the exalted branch
Of anthems ancient and true
Amidst rustling leaves of longing
And flowering blooms of beauty,
Pink and white, crimson red,
Moved by meandering winds
And gentle zephyrs of eternal mystery,
Trill with undying fervor, unabated zeal,
Timeless ecstasy and faithful devotion,
Your mystic songs of love
That your beauteous melodies
Transcend bird and cloud,

Take flight and soar
In the heavenly, beckoning skies
Of the ardent heart and luminous soul.

Nightingale,
When you nest,
May it be
In the rose gardens of eternity
Folded deep within
The hallowed precincts
Of the illumined heart,
That your holy, immaculate warbling
Bring to life, unfold, lay bear,
Untold realities latent,
Eager to emerge, shine as heavenly light
By dint of your song.

Nightingale,
We long to hear
Your sweet melodies
That the songbirds of our souls
Take them to heart,
Press them to our bosom,
Recite their resounding missives
Of ancient truths
And burgeoning spiritual light
In the perfumed gardens
Of passionate search and inner meanings
Situated on the verdant slopes
And flowering hillsides
Of the spirit,
Where,
Freed from worldly desire

And released from the fetters
Of self-love and ignoble pursuits,
The soul finds joy, abiding peace,
Bliss and happiness.

Nightingale,
In the sanctified realms
Of our inmost reality
May our hearts be pure, our souls sincere,
That your sweet, vivifying melodies
Enrapture our souls,
Lift us to the great beyond
Where angels fly and cherubs play
Then swoon away in prayer,
That we may,
Enamored birds of the spirit,
Soar in joy and delight
The ineffable paradise within,
Glide long and true,
On heavenly winds of contentment,
Then ride,
As moonlight rides the night,
Mighty gales of wonderment
And sweeping winds of spirituality,
Love and kindness.

Nightingale,
Warble once again
And from the rose garden
Of your being,
Your ethereal melodies
That we may ascend

To the illimitable empyrean
Of the holy and the sacred,
Behold the timeless firmament
Of manifest light
Beaming from the Sun of Reality,
That its warming rays
Kindle a flame,
Set ablaze
The inmost torch of love,
Its fiery flames ordained
To burn to ash the dross of self
As the sun turns to naught
Primordial darkness.
And then,
Souls fully alive, on fire,
Hearts blazing and illumined,
May we surrender
To the divine within,
The Divine without.

Such are the retreats of the spirit
Longing lovers search for.
Such are the realms of the heart
They quest.
Such is the journey of the soul
For impassioned lovers
Who seek,
No matter the cost,
The mystic warbling
And transcendent songs
Of the Nightingale of love,
Its rapturous trilling
A call
To all mankind.

Might This I Be?

A lover,
Might this I be?
For neither scholar nor seer
Am I,
Nor will I ever be.
Sagacity and wisdom
Lie well outside my pale,
And great intellect and capacity
Have never been my lot.
All these fly far too high
For my small, unremarkable
Wings of soul
To aspire to,
To reach.

My gifts,
Humble few that they are,
One and all,
Are far too ordinary
To shine brightly,
Or even shine at all,
In those lofty realms!

But a lover
Of all peoples,
Of all that is good,
All that is holy,
Of every soul,
Every righteous thought

And kindly act,
This is what
I wish to be!

Greatness and fame,
Grandiosity,
Wealth and riches,
Notoriety and acclaim,
These hold no interest
For me,
For I see them
As a passing wind
Crossing a barren desert
Surrendering,
In the end,
To the cutting cold of night
And scorching heat
Of despair and loneliness,
Of fleeting fancies.

But should it be
His pleasure –
And for this I pray –
And should I wholeheartedly strive,
My heart pure,
My intention good,
And should I stay the course
And struggle long,
Then, maybe,
Just maybe,
And to my heart's delight,
A humble savant
Of love
I might be.

My Canvas Is The Page

I heard a poet
Lamenting to wind and flower,
Rustling leaves and cooing doves
Eager to listen:

My canvas is the page,
It calls to me,
The caressing touch of the pen,
The sensuous warmth of flowing ink,
The blush of color,
Words of love and rapture
To dance across throbbing hearts,
Shine with joy
In the mystic orb
Of the soul.

The page,
Lonely,
Long ignored,
Beckons pen and ink
For verse
To illuminate, dazzle, enlighten,
Soar with eagles,
Dive with preying falcons,
Transcend the desert sands
Of the mundane.

Unsatisfied,
It cries aloud

For flames of truth
To quench the gloom
Of the bleak passages of life,
Illumine the journey of the soul,
Reveal gemlike treasures
Of mind and thought
Hidden deep within
Faith and reason.

Wanting more,
It dreams of verse
To intrigue, capture,
Excite the imagination –
Mountain peaks and snow-capped summits
Of lofty themes;
Powerful rivers and mighty falls
Of rushing reflection;
Murmuring brooks
And caressing, meandering streams
Of softly flowing sincerity;
Gardens of hyacinth and rose
Sweetly scented in delicate shades of beauty;
Hills of cherry blossoms
Perfumed in bursting pink and white,
Their petals
Magical ballerinas dancing rhapsodically
In winds of joy and delight;
Fanciful birds of flight
In poetic skies
Of wonderment and beauty.

My brush is the pen,
Strong and eager, ever hopeful,

Yet weary of hand,
Burdened by chagrin,
Disappointment and incapacity.
Swiftly it slips away,
Unfulfilled, unrequited,
Sad and forlorn,
To repose in the inkwell
Of hope and promise!

My palette is word and line
Inspired by ineffable colors
Of light and glory,
Majesty and breathtaking beauty
Bequeathed by Nature.
Oh, to write
As She paints! –
With depth of space and breadth of time,
Images strong, verse that rhymes,
The unfolding of the seasons,
Blooms of spring,
Ripened fruits of summer!

Canvas, pen and ink
Reside within,
Flow from heart and mind.
Therein,
Poets live and dream,
Strive and struggle.
Therein,
The journey of verse
Has no end
And the pursuit of poetry,
Restless and alive

To truth, beauty and love
Lives on.

The poetic path
Is stony and rough
And word and verse
Stumble and falter across the page.
Still,
Should some passerby linger,
See shades of beauty,
Textures of depth or meaning;
Or flights of thought
To traverse meadows within,
And the far reaches
Of the soul's supernal skies;
Or that blow
As a summer night's breeze
In the lavender-scented garden
Of the heart;
Then the poet,
Renewed, hope revived,
Will, once again,
Reach for canvas, brush and palette,
And paint,
As best he can,
Portraits of enduring love
And scenes of subtle beauty,
Landscapes of gushing truth,
And poetic images
To thrill the eye,
Enchant the soul.

And,
Should the pen be kind,
The ink willing,
The page receptive,
Then, perhaps,
Will verse and rhyme,
Humble though they be,
Stand the ancient tests
Of beauty, meaning,
And,
Most especially,
Time.

New Fallen Snow

Reflections on the Word of God on a cold Wisconsin winter day

New fallen snow
Descended
From Heaven's Bounty,
Falls upon waiting,
Outstretched branches
Of my soul,
Each branch reaching out
In unworthy praise
Of the Sun of Truth.

Water of Life
Pure,
Hydrates
The arid soil
Of my being,
Renews hope, perseverance,
Joy
And possibilities
Of transformation –
These yield quietude,
Solace
And peace.

Once more,
Determined, preparing to arise,
I rest in the outstretched arms
Of His Love,

Revived
From Words
Heaven sent,
Soft,
Life-giving,
Like new fallen snow.

O Land of Nightingale and Rose!

*In honor and remembrance of young women whose lives have
been lost to, or stolen by, oppression, cruelty and death*

O land of nightingale and rose!
I perceive not from easterly winds
The sweet perfume of blooming rose
Nor the heavenly redolence of hyacinth
Wafting from once-fragrant gardens.

Might it be that your maidens
Of blooming promise,
Young, fragrant and fresh,
Have been cut down and cast aside
In the prime of youth
And budding womanhood?

I think it must be so,
For I hear cries of sorrow
And repression,
Poignant calls for equality,
Freedom and justice
Carried on those self-same winds.

What compels you,
O ancient,
Once-proud land of poets,
Blessed and honored by the Beloved,
To cut down, violate
God's precious flowers

In the rose gardens of His love?
Is not life their God-given right?
Has He not created these very flowers
To spread their fragrant petals,
Perfume the land and its peoples,
Adorn the pages of time
With the redolent essence
Of their lives?

And what of the sweet hyacinth
Of the spirit
Once wafted from budding hearts and souls?
What of the enchanting melodies,
Now forever lost,
Never to be sung or played?
What of the dreams once dreamed
For an enlightened, emancipated tomorrow?
Would that these easterly winds,
Perfumed in flowering hyacinth,
Carry all of these,
But, alas,
Their missive
Is but loss and lamentation,
The crushing oppression
Of generations.

O land of warbling nightingales
And beauteous roses,
Do you not hear the call of God and humanity,
Louder than cathedral bells
And the call to prayer,
For dignity, equality,
The right to life?

It is these,
Not shackles of oppression
And fettering chains
That please the Beloved,
He Who gives breath and wing
To all creation.

O maidens,
Be assured!
Have no doubt!
The unfailing Hand of God
Will set you free from shackle and chain,
Raise you high in skies of light and glory
To claim your rightful place
In sublime heavens of liberty,
Equality and respect.

And though the din of injustice
Echoes loud,
Still,
In quiet moments and upon the winds,
Can be heard, unrestrained and true,
The tale of the beauty, courage, daring and faith
That are yours.
And upon rushing gales of hope and victory
Can be heard the irrepressible cry,
"Fear not!
Be not dismayed!
For your glorious destiny,
Like the unfolding of the rose
And the fragrance of hyacinth,
Is promised and assured!"

One Humanity, Two Wings

Two Doves,
One male,
One female,
At peace, build their nest as one.

Two swans,
One male,
One female,
Live, swim as one.

Two nightingales,
One male,
One female,
Charm, charmed by, the same rose.

Two robins,
One male,
One female,
Fly as one.

Two songbirds,
One male,
One female,
Upon the branch, sing sweet, ancestral song.

Two eagles,
One male,
One female,
Soar high in the same heavens.

One humanity,
Two wings,
One male,
One female;
With equality,
This bird,
Too,
Will fly,
Soar aloft,
Captivate the heavens,
Sing songs of love and peace
Written, scored for,
The ages.

One Planet, Two Worlds

One planet,
Two worlds,
Division in the middle.

One globe,
Rich,
Poor,
Struggle in the middle.

One Earth,
Fertile, coherent,
Ravaged, exploited,
Uncertainty in the middle.

One planet,
Two worlds,
Hope in the middle.

One humanity,
One destiny,
Love in the middle.

Patience

Patience,
Quiet beauty,
How you elude us so!
Your beauty, we know well,
So pure and free of mere sensuality.
Your allure cannot be denied.
Your rare charm beguiles.
Your godliness is to be revered,
Aspired to.

Patience,
How we desire you!
Fill our hearts!
Teach us your ways!
Instruct us day by day!
Romance us with your sweet smile,
Loving kindness, softly spoken words!
Assure us through your endless serenity,
Timeless composure!

Patience,
Beloved maiden,
If this be too much to ask,
Then,
And should you deign it so,
Warm our hearts with your beauty!
Fill our souls with your dignity and strength!
Cause our tongues, ever impatient,
To obey your every command!

Patience,
Handmaiden of the Eternal,
Goddess from the Divine,
How we admire you,
Wish to emulate, be, all that you are!
But, alas,
The peaceful, disciplined heavens you fly in,
The tempered skies you soar in,
Still remain far above the reach
Of our tattered,
Feeble wings!

Peaks of Grandeur

A Reflection on the Rocky Mountains

Peaks of grandeur
Bathed in illumination,
Tributes to the one Creator,
Majestic,
Prominent,
Imagined in time before time,
Fashioned from power and glory,
Twin descendants
Of God's Holy Word –
Rise high,
Shout your praise of Him,
The Unknowable!

Towering giants
Humbled before Omniscience
And Omnipresence,
Grandiose symbols of obedience
To deigned teleology,
Unshakable,
Unmovable,
Inimitable in the past,
Unrivaled in the present,
You stand for all eternity
An undying testimony
To the Hand that shaped you
And carved your beauty.

Purity

Purity,
Heavenly maiden,
Beloved damsel of the Divine,
How I long for a glimpse
Of your transcendent beauty,
To glance upon your raven locks,
To gaze, but for a moment,
Deep into your telling, lucent eyes!

Yet,
I dare not
Even the slightest attempt
To behold the comely radiance
Of your smile,
The sanctified glow
Of your lovely brow,
For my eyes,
Unaccustomed to such godliness,
Strangers to such beauty fair,
And undeserving of your gaze,
Refuse my longing heart
Even the merest glance
Of your lovely countenance.

Though all this be true,
Still, I yearn,
Deep within my soul,
For all that you are,
All that,

In your hands and by your power,
I might be,
Can become!

I long to know you
As moonlight knows the dark of night,
As vernal flowers know the rain,
As the soaring bird knows flight,
As the cooing dove knows songs soft and sweet.
I yearn for us to be as one,
Even as bride and groom celebrating their nuptials,
To be your adoring, unfailing consort
On the glimmering pathways of eternity,
Your lover –
For you are my beloved! –
In the rose gardens and tulip fields
Of the placeless,
The high mountains and surging seas
Of an ever-unfolding spirituality.

My heart cries out,
Yearning to walk
The sanctified avenues of wonderment,
Hand in hand, heart in heart,
Beneath brilliant supernal skies,
Your luminous, breathtaking reality
Illuminating my soul, edifying my being!
I long to dwell in the flower garden
Of happiness and contentment with you,
Sing your praises, extol you name,
Write verse to please you!

And might we,
O purity,
Traverse the heavens,
Every sphere and all that vibrates,
And then enter every paradise
Upon waves of holy light powered by the Divine,
He Who is All-Powerful, All-Bountiful?
And if all this we might do,
Then let us dance,
Lover and beloved,
United as one, eternally close,
Upon blowing winds of faith and faithfulness,
Across the wiles of today
And the promise of endless tomorrows!

Purity,
Damsel divine,
I pray,
Nay, beg you!
Forgive my bold, unwelcome speech,
My rash, assuming nature,
For, in truth,
And as you, yourself, will testify,
Bear witness
Before all who are in heaven and on earth,
I have no right to call you by name,
Address you in crass, feeble lines that ashamed,
Weep and cry upon the page,
That sadden the pen and beg the ink
No longer flow.

Still,
Crazed lover that I am,

I cannot, will not, deny
My love and admiration for you,
Neither my burning devotion
And adoration for all that you are!
Your shining countenance,
Your rising dawn within my being,
Brighter than noontide glory,
Has captivated my soul!
Your presence,
A lamp to illuminate my being,
Humbles the great, endless orbs
God, alone, can reckon,
Shines as an example for those who love,
Those who trust,
Those who pledge fealty one to another,
Those who live a good and godly life.

Transcendent beauty,
Should it please you,
And for this I truly pray,
Take my hand! Lead the way!
Bestow true life! Purify my soul!
Fill my heart with your magical elixir,
My soul with the radiance of your being,
My mind and thought
With your softly flowing, murmuring,
Limpid waters of meaning and purpose!

Angelic purity,
Have mercy on my soul!
Burn to ash my tattered robe of self,
For it no longer suits me!
Cleanse my heart of the dross within –

Conflagration of the soul that it is! –
Lest it consume me,
My soul perish in its deadly fire,
And my dreams and aspirations
Be but short-lived, dying embers
In the barren wastelands and deserted haunts
Of the unrepentant and lost.

Cast away,
O mystical maiden,
In His Name and for His love,
All ungodliness within me!
And, then,
Should it be His pleasure
That you deign it so,
Take my life and take my hand,
Purify my heart and enlighten my soul,
For then,
And only then,
Will I dare to look upon
The timeless, delicate beauty that is yours,
Gaze deep into your luminous eyes,
And utter these words that my heart cries out to say:
"Beloved maiden,
Cherished damsel of the Divine,
Walk as one
The avenues of life with me!
Sail as one
The seas of love with me!
Dive as one
The oceans of understanding and wisdom with me!
Fly as one
The skies of the spirit with me!

Beloved maiden,
Blessed reality born
Of the most pure breath of God,
I, with all my heart and soul,
All my being, all that I am,
Do love you so!
My heart is ablaze for you!
My spirit, on fire, calls to you!
My hopes –
Endlessly streaming like the zephyrs of spring
That woo daffodil and crocus,
And the gentle breezes of summer
That thrill tree and pond –
Are that we,
You and I,
Forever,
With joy and gladness
And locked in close embrace,
The truest and purest of lovers,
Be as one,
Never, ever to part,
And my eyes,
Though ever unworthy
Of the splendor of your loveliness,
For all time and across the ages,
Gaze into the hallowed sanctity
Of yours!"

Purpose and Reality Embrace

Purpose and Reality
Embrace
And dance among the stars,
Ethereal zephyrs
Untethered to space
And time,
With choreography
Transcendent,
Step and form
Mingled
In unrehearsed
Beauty,
Giving birth
To emergent expressions
Of oneness,
Complexity
And order.

Adorned in Design,
Long-legged,
Graceful,
Tantalizing,
Passionate expressions
Of ultimate outcomes,
Informed by zeal
And force,
They move
Amongst the stars,
But within the souls,

Dancing sacred,
Resplendent
Steps of Truth,
Awakening seeking hearts,
Illuminating vital minds.
The negligent and shallow
Remain unawakened,
The performance,
Dazzling,
Eternal,
Invisible
In their darkness.

Purpose and Reality
Embrace
And dance among the stars
And within our souls,
Moving on waves
Of Inspiration
And Revelation.
Mystery and the Plain
Are their two-step
As they whirl
Through ceaseless generations.
To unfold these
Is to unfold all.

Questing Paths

Quest in search of gay frivolity
If you must.

Walk the avenues of elusive dreams
If that be your goal.

Traverse the desert sands of ephemeral delights
If shifting sands you wish to tread.

But expect not lasting joy and enduring pleasure,
Abiding love and undisturbed peace.

For these,
One must walk the questing paths
Of love and justice, generosity and godliness.

It is then
That peace and tranquility are given,
Joy and happiness bestowed,
Illumination of the heart realized,
The soul enkindled –
All these abiding in depths within,
Pearls of lustrous beauty
Undisturbed
By the moving currents and crashing waves,
Rising tides and billowing waters,
Of the great sea of life.

Rapture

Rapture,
Hold me tight in your grasp,
Close to your bosom
And closer still,
That the ecstasy of your vintage wine
Thrill me,
Intoxicate my soul
For all time.

Fling me high
To where angels fly
And holy souls gather and pray,
Where the sun of love,
Brilliant, magnificent,
Never sets,
And darkness,
Contrary to this nether world,
Never follows day.

Take me to lofty realms
Beyond cloud and star,
That I might traverse the heavens,
Soar and glide on beams of streaming light,
Explore mystic depths within,
In truth and meaning
Find delight.

Rapture,
I am yours!

Do with me as you please,
For life's journey on this mortal plane
Is short,
And there is no time
To lose!

Ripples on the Pond

Ripples on the pond,
What tales of love
Flowing
From the bosom of your rippling waters,
Have you to tell?

What whisperings from dancing winds
To illumine Nature's scrolls and poems
Flow through you,
Those awaiting seer and sage,
The spiritually enlightened,
To unravel beneath brilliant, revealing lights
Of wisdom and understanding?
Are they whisperings of a New Day
Of peace, oneness?
For this we hope!

What songs
From the breasts of caroling larks
And warbling nightingales
Played on strings of meandering winds,
Flute and lute of gentle breeze,
Do you present to amorous, admiring shores?
Are they songs of the spirit
From ineffable, supernal realms,
Ancient melodies of the heart
Enraptured lovers shield in their breasts,
Intone in rhapsodic song
In the grand concert hall of the soul?

If this be true,
Let us hear them now!

Ripples on the pond,
Your serenity and calm,
Intimate communion with springtime zephyrs,
Summer winds,
Can not be denied!
From where do these flow?
From what pure fountains
Do they spring forth?
Tell us now
That these move and flow,
Through us, too!

Perfumed
By frolicking breezes
Wafting fragrances of hyacinth,
Jasmine and rose,
You offer these to sky and shore,
Freely and without expectation,
A humble offering to those you love.
Such generosity,
We, too, must learn!

Like the devoted lover
Whose rendezvous with his best-beloved
Is not to be denied,
You move unhesitatingly,
Free of doubt,
To pond's edge,
Where ripple and shore,
Lover and beloved,

Tryst,
Proclaim everlasting fealty.
In this are lessons for the infatuated
And the young,
The betrothed,
Those on the gale-ravaged precipice
Of infidelity.

Ripples on the pond,
You inspire profundity and reflection.
What wisdoms do you unfold
To edify heart and soul?
Ancient truths,
Pond-born ballerinas consigned to your care,
Move and dance with you,
Perform on the moving stage
Of rhythmic waters,
Give light
To the dance of the soul.

Truly,
Nature loves you so!
Birds of flight and beasts of the field
Visit often,
Confirm your rightful place
In the grand scheme
Born of the womb of Mother Nature.
Falling rain and brilliant sun
Are drawn to you.
Playful springtime zephyrs
And sprightly summer breezes
Love you, too!

These bear gifts
Of sundry blossom and flower!

Ripples on the pond,
You forever delight the hopelessly romantic,
Inspire the poet's aspiring, searching pen,
Give hope to the forgotten,
Quiet the heart of the longing lover.
How salubrious your visage!
How faithful to your entrusted tasks!

Assuredly,
The heavens love you,
For as the lingering sun sets
And the sky smiles broadly
In shades of orange, gold and red,
The rising moon greets you
With shining beams of moonglow,
And the quiet of the night,
Unwilling you be left alone,
Draws close,
Reflects,
As do you,
On life and day.
So many lessons you teach!
So few the hearts that contemplate,
Understand!

And in the morn
When night draws to a close
And the awakened sun rises,
You gleam once again in story and tale,
Windswept song,

And propelled by breaths
From the lungs of Creation
And mindful of duty,
You make your way,
As you always have,
To adoring shores.

All this,
Humanity has yet to learn.
When we do,
Goodwill and kindness,
Blown by revelatory winds
From the Eternal,
Will ripple on the ponds of our hearts
And flow as mighty waves
On a surging sea
To transformative shores
Of joy and peace,
Tranquility and love,
One world, one people!

River of Life

I heard a man
Sitting by a river
Muse on the days of his life.
These are the words he spoke:

River of life,
My heart has questions
It must ask.
My soul has answers
It must know.
Let us, then,
Muse as one
Before the final setting of the sun,
Its glorious rise to be no more,
And the winds of this nether life
Cease to blow.

Have we drifted long,
Without meaning,
Purpose eluding us,
Or have we moved
With salubrious winds
And gentle gales,
Well-wishers
To young and old,
A solace
To the heavy of heart?

On our journey,
Did we encounter truth,
Hold it close
As your banks and bed
Hold your waters,
Or did we pass it by,
Too consumed in our own lives
To notice,
Pay it any heed,
Thinking truth but rock and stone
Encountered
Along the way?

Did we welcome,
Take as our own,
Pure waters from lofty,
Icy mountain streams
Of the spirit
That we be pure of soul
And pure of heart?
Did we seek understanding
From empowering thundering falls
Of thought and mind,
Profundity
From your depths?

What ancient
Whisperings of wisdom
From murmuring brooks,
And kindly exhortations
From gentle rains
And springtime showers
Gifted

From watchful clouds on high,
Did we welcome,
Make our own,
Offer
To those with ear to hear,
Heart to listen,
Soul to grasp?

Have our days been warm,
Sunlit and bright,
Our evenings quiet, serene?
Have the sunrises of our years
Been harbingers
Of ever better, brighter days,
Their sunsets
Breathtaking confirmation
Of days well spent?

Have the risings of the moon
Born witness
To the rising light
Of love and kindness
In the heavens of our heart,
The skies of our soul,
Or has that light remained low,
A fallen orb,
Reluctant,
Unwilling to rise?

And what of life's twists and turns?
Have we navigated them well?
Have we gently caressed
Your faithful, loving banks

With the softness,
The gratitude and tender affection
They deserve?

Did we give due consideration
To life's blowing winds
That came our way?
Did they linger long,
Refresh our soul,
Tell us tales
Of beauty and hope,
Breathe life
Into the book
Of hidden mysteries?

Did those winds recite verse
To lay bare
Spiritual realities
Latent deep within?
Did we learn them then?
Can we recite them now,
Or are they long forgotten,
Forgotten quite?

So many gentle breezes
Of opportunity
Greeted us,
Encouraged us on our way!
Did we honor them,
Do the same for others?
Have we moved on streaming flows
Of love, solicitude,
A voice raised high and long for justice?

Did we speak out
On behalf of the beleaguered,
The oppressed?

River of life,
We have journeyed long!
Tell me, truly,
As truly as we are one!
Have I danced across your waters
Or merely meandered across the years?
Have I squandered precious time
Or used my days well?
Have I given freely, selflessly,
Or was I filled with self and pride?
Did I hold life close and fast
Or lose it along the way?

After a long silence
The river seemed to say,

O sojourner
On the river of life!
O my friend!
Truly,
Life has been kind,
And you have shown it
Every kindness,
Shared every goodness!
Let us, then,
Be on our way,
Our hearts light, our spirits gay,
For days of joy and love,
Laughter and cheer,

Await us,
And our journey,
Eternal,
Is long from over!

Sea of Light

Sea of Light,
Radiant,
Splendorous,
Emitting glory
From ethereal drops,
Water the desolate shores
Where human life struggles
Towards nobility.
Our parched hearts yearn
For your vitalizing Elixir.
Let it flow through us,
And to all mankind.

Illumine the dark,
Desolate passages
Of our dimmed lives,
Water our desiccated souls,
Gush out in rising tides of wisdom
And cresting waves of hope
To fill our beings
And light our way
To the Fashioner
Of all Light.
He seeks us,
And we seek Him.

Sea of Light,
Eternal Ocean
Of His Command,

Transform our souls
Into salubrious streams
Descending from high mountain passes,
Coursing through hill and valley,
Village and town,
City and heart,
Relentlessly rushing
To the Eternal,
Glorious Sea
From whence they came
And for which they yearn,
Its eager waters
Awaiting them.

The Mighty Seed of Love

A short story cast in the form of verse

A wise old sage,
Hearing those around him
Lamenting the condition of the world,
And after reflecting on their comments,
Wisely said,

"A cruel world
Is as hard ground and a thorny branch,
A cold heart is as stone."

When asked,
"If this is so,
How do we make the world
A better place?
What is it that we can do?",
He thoughtfully replied,

"A kindly heart
Is as a summer breeze,
A loving heart as a gentle rain.

A caring soul
Is as the sweetness of honey,
A sincere smile as springtime.

True friendship
Is as cooing doves and warbling nightingales,
Its timeless bond as the melodies they sing.

Gentle words
Are as the breath of life to a beating heart,
As joy and laughter to the life of a child.

Generosity and compassion
Are as billowing waves
To quench parched and forgotten sands,
As lustrous pearls of the spirit
Cast upon the shores of the grieving heart.

Patience and restraint
Are as sunshine and flowers to the soul,
As moonlight to the newly betrothed.

Words of wisdom
Are as nectar to the butterfly,
As sunrise to the morn and all that lives and moves.

Encouragement and understanding
Are are as murmuring brooks and meandering streams
To water the lives of those we meet,
As rushing rivers
To quench the thirst of the seeking soul."

After these
And many other words of wisdom,
He concluded,

"All of this must spring forth
From the mighty seed of love
Planted in the rose garden of the heart
By the All-Loving, the All-Bountiful –
It is ours to protect it, ours to cultivate it,

To nurture its shining ruby petals,
Release its sublime essence."

The wise old sage briefly paused
And then continued,

"But, most importantly,
Love must be shared lavishly with others.
It must perfume every space and clime
And waft across
The hearts and souls of all peoples
As a summer breeze
Gently wafts across hill and vale,
Thorn and flower,
Barren desert and fruitful trees,
And always,
Without exception!"

Seize Me!

Dreams
To thrill the soul where love,
Enthralled angelic dancer,
Slides across Heaven's sky in praise of the Beloved –
Seize me!

Dreams
To sweeten the trampled, challenged lives of the oppressed,
More sweet than dripping troves
Of summer's delectable amber –
Seize me!

Dreams
Of hearts pulsating loving and tender care
For creatures great and small,
For every soul,
In the bosom of resolute solicitude
For all that lives and moves and breathes –
Seize me!

Dreams
To calm the frantic and frenetic,
Reassure the dispossessed, the struggling,
Soothe weary and despairing souls in tumultuous times –
Seize me!

Dreams
Of goddesses good and grand champions of hope and altruism,
Of faith and certitude

That revive, enkindle, empower the downtrodden –
Seize me!

Dreams
To arise, transform, be more than we are, all that we might be,
That our lives, well-spent, be of some small worth,
And our journey's end be without regret –
Seize me!

Dreams
Of a forged destiny on the Anvil of the Unseen,
Of abiding unity and long-lived justice,
Of peace and harmony,
Of undeniable love and ineffable beauty –
Seize me!

Dreams,
Times are hard, injustices heavy, difficult to bear.
Peoples suffer, seek refuge from their agonizing plight.
Challenges are daunting
And people of good will everywhere need you,
One and all,
As do I,
To spur us on!

Seize My Soul

Seize my soul,
That I be free.

Seize my heart,
That I might love.

Seize my mind,
That knowledge dwell within.

Seize my sight,
That I might see.

Seize my hearing
That I hear again.

Seize all that I am,
Lest I perish,
Lost and forlorn
On the plain of self,
And the journey of life
Be walked in vain,
A desolate path,
A road forsaken.

Self

Simple verse cast in brevity and rhyme

Self,
Begetter of arrogance and pride,
The wise bade you leave
Long ago,
Sought to cast you out,
Bring you low.

Still,
How you linger,
Prance about!
Now,
It is ours to slay you,
Of this,
Be assured,
Have no doubt!

The battle of the soul is waged in the heart.
With sharpened sword, arrows of might,
Let us slay the darkness!
Dwell in brilliant, selfless light!

Serenity

Serenity,
Fair maiden
Of quiet beauty,
Your lovely visage
Gives rise
To sunlit morns of heart and soul,
Murmuring brooks of the mind,
Windswept whispers that perfume
The reality within,
Soothe the grand illusion
Without.

Beloved maiden,
How sweet
Your softly spoken words,
The melody of your speech!
They call to mind
The cooing of a dove
High in the tree of tranquility,
The warbling of the nightingale
Lost in wonderment
In the rapturous presence
Of the many-petaled rose.

Your glance,
Soft as moonglow,
Inspires calm assurance
Deep in the hearts of lovers,
Brings to mind

The delicate, flirting touch of the Monarch
Fluttering, flower to flower,
Until it lights upon
The purple-pink 'Cinderella'
It loves so well,
There to rendezvous
In brilliant, bold color
With its sweet, delectable nectar,
Confess before land and sky
And without shame,
Undying devotion.

The touch
Of your hand in mine,
Reminiscent of springtime
Softly flowing across garden and pond,
Brightly flowered avenues,
The cheek of a newborn babe
Held close
In the loving arms of its mother,
I cannot describe.
Only the heart,
With the flowing ink
Of heavenly peace and luminous tranquility,
Can pen such tender, transcendent sentiments,
And then,
Only on the rolled out parchment
Of its own self.

Serenity,
How you do amaze!
And how I love you so!
Come!

Sit by my side!
Linger awhile,
Perhaps even for a lifetime!
Tell me tales of long ago
And tales of times to come.

Beloved maiden,
My deepest wish,
The longing of my soul,
Is to forever have you near,
For, I am,
Alas,
Unresigned
That we should part,
Unwilling
To let you go!

Should Have, Could Have

Should have,
Could have,
Didn't.

Would have,
Could have,
Didn't.

Such is a life poorly lived,
A lesson for all
Who still have
Time.

Soft Blush of Reason

Soft blush of reason,
Red in the flush of love,
Whisper in my soul
Truths,
Yesterday,
I could not bear.
May they ring out
To my every atom
In bell-like tones,
Lest my hearing
Pay them no mind.

Tender flowing thoughts
Coursing
Through the riverbeds
Of my mind,
Strangers yesterday,
Embraced today,
Hasten your currents
To the spirit's crystal pond
Where goodness takes root
And charity grows.
For too long,
I have been indifferent.
There is much to know
And I have but eternity.

Vision,
Newly bestowed,

Blinded
Before the brilliance
Of the Ethereal Sun,
Acute
In Its light,
Open wide the eyes
Of my humanity.
Realities,
Once imprisoned in shadows
And chained to darkness
Are released into illumination
Amidst glorious
Pulsations
Of profundity and wisdom.

Soft blush of reason,
Red in the flush of love,
Tell my heart
Of the new mysteries,
Revealed and sound,
That in it
All reason may be swept away,
And only the Beloved
Found.

Softly Flowing Waters

Softly flowing waters
Meander into lovers' hearts
Where love alone
Can shape a stream's bed.

Amidst pastures of purity
And green, rolling hills of faith,
The lovers find joy
In remembrance of their Beloved.

The winds whisper His name
Over mountains and hillsides.
The valleys, lakes and ponds
Hear this, too.

Birds warble melodies,
Gentle, serene,
That fill the air
And touch the heart,
But can not climb
Into the heaven
Of His song,
Where melody glistens
And harmonies take form
From strings and horns of light.

Limpid waters from gurgling brooks
Lap onto ground's edge,
Where flowers grow and lovers walk,

Yearning to emulate the life-giving Words
That water the blossoming gardens
Of His lovers' hearts.
Their gay, splashing drops,
Infused with the story of His love,
Course as endlessly as His bounty.

To those who revel in Him,
All creation is but His shadow,
A reflection of His glory,
A portal to behold His visasge.
For them, the universe unfolded
Blazons His Name
In paeans of triumph
And explosions of birth.

For His lovers,
Their hearts illumined,
Their souls afire
With His light,
All else is darkness
And can find no entry.
The Beloved walks beside them,
His voice beauteous,
His presence unmistakable.
He is their only goal.
They can abide no other.

Sorrow and Joy Embrace

Sorrow and joy,
Such a tale you tell,
One that resonates across the ages,
Worthy, in truth, to be retold:

Joy,
Brilliant light
From sunlit skies,
Descends on beams
Of grace and bounty.
Sorrow,
Even as morning fog,
Rises from the inhumanity
Of the living,
The ill words and works
Of the dead.
These,
Sorrow and joy,
Dance heart and soul,
The quiet –
Or tormented –
Avenues of remembrance
And reflection.

Joy
Dances to rhythms
Of love and learning,
Wonder and contentment,
Feelings too sweet to pen,

Too luminous for ink and page.
Unafraid
Of mighty gales
Of challenge and change,
Welcoming gentle breezes
Perfumed in gifts of spring,
Joy,
Unrestrained,
Dances atop
The capricious winds of life
With assurance,
Unfeigned delight.

Sorrow,
Unable to rise,
Move upon the winds,
Dances the unlit streets
And alleyways
Of loss and cruelty,
Ill-spent passions
And unrequited love.
Dark,
Unpaved roads of injustice,
Oppression and tyranny
Know well
Its muddled dance.

Sorrow and joy,
Disparate dancers,
Reluctant partners,
Embrace,
Dance as one
In heart and soul

Across the stage of life.
Choice and circumstance,
Intention and judgment
Determine the music they dance to –
And more importantly,
Which one leads!

Springtime

Springtime,
How faithful you are!
Even as the summer breeze
You return year after year,
And as the rose
Of felicity and beauty
Blooms in the garden
Of the bosom of young love,
So do you,
With power and grace,
Spring forth and flower
Across hill and vale,
Mountainside and meadow,
Bringing joy and mirth,
Once again,
To gladden,
Bring cheer,
Thrill
All creation.

Springtime,
It is you
Who gives voice
To nesting songbirds,
The calling whistle of the meadowlark.
It is you
Who causes
Primrose and tulips to bloom
And hyacinth, petal by petal,

To rejoice,
Set free
Its God-given, heavenly redolence
Into welcoming winds
Impatient to release
That quintessential, inspired perfume,
Even as alluring melodies
Are impatient to be released
From lute and harp,
Warbling nightingales.
Unrestrained as the meandering,
Zealous zephyrs carrying them,
Each fragrant note of those melodies
Seeks its vernal rendezvous
With butterflies and bumble bees,
Honeysuckle and sunlight,
Springtime lovers who,
Hand in hand,
And whisper by whisper,
Vow eternal fealty,
Lifelong devotion.

And springtime,
How faithful
Your delicate, queenly daffodils!
Mounted high atop
Their lofty verdant thrones
They return each year
To the rhythms of nature,
Ever so quietly
And with the utmost humility.
How lonely they must have felt,
Far from your warm embracing arms

And youthful tender bosom
During the cold of winter.
How lonely
Must have been those nights
When, sleeping quietly,
They dreamed endlessly
Of caressing breezes,
Softly flowing murmuring brooks,
Gentle springtime showers,
Rustling leaves and chirping birds,
The call of the whippoorwill.
How they,
And all your flowers,
Eager to bloom,
Must have yearned
For the dawning of your vernal sun
And sunlit days!

Springtime,
You will dwell in our hearts forever!
Though howling winds
And mighty gales may blow,
Though harsh winter nights may come,
Flaunt their cold and linger long,
Though winter days
Be gray and uninviting,
Nonetheless,
We, and all that is –
All creation! –
Will forever await you –
Steadfast lovers
Of the endless charm and song,
Beauty and florescence

That is yours to give,
And that you so bountifully share,
Generously and without fail,
Spring after spring.

Standing Before the Pathways of Life

At the threshold of intention
Which will we choose,
Sincerity and purity
Or selfish motivation?

At the altars of good and evil,
Which will we honor?
Before which will we pray?

At the crossroads of kindliness and cruelty,
Caring and indifference,
Which direction will we walk? –
To the flowering vale of contentment
Or to the murky abyss of unhappiness and discontent?

Standing before the pathways of life,
Which path will we tread?
The path of love and concord
Or the path of disdain and division?

To answer the last question
Is to answer all the rest!
Better, then,
That we choose wisely!

Supreme Antidote

Envy –
Deep hole in the soul.

Vainglory –
Chasm of trampled ash.

Pride –
Stony bottom of destruction.

Vanity –
Slough of delusion.

Self-righteousness,
Black pit of no return.

Love of self –
Stygian gorge of death.

Love of God,
Humility before all –
Supreme antidote!

Take My Hand

Take my hand if yours is weak.
My grasp is strong, I will not let go.

If your heart is weak, fear not,
For mine is strong, it will beat for both of us.

Should your breath fail, your words be weak,
Be not concerned, for my voice is strong
And I will speak for both of us.

Walk with me.
If your legs be weak and your back frail,
It is of no account.
I will lift you up and carry you,
For I am strong and will not let you fall.

Trust in me as I trust in you,
For I see the Path you seek, long for.
I walk it still, know it well,
And can show you the way.

The Deep Look Within

The deep look within –
Light for one soul,
Darkness for another.

Tenderness and compassion for one soul,
Cold stone for another.

Still ponds for one soul,
Turbulent seas for another.

The deep look within –
Joy and gaiety for one soul,
Sadness and despair for another.

Trilling songbirds for one soul,
Fire-breathing dragons for another.

Green fields of flowering selflessness for one soul,
Barren, murky bottoms of self for another.

The deep look within –
Flourishing gardens of lilac, honeysuckle, hyacinth and rose for
one soul,
Arid lands of blowing sands for another.

Paeans of gratitude for one soul,
The broken harp of regret for another.

The deep look within –
When the sun sets on the days of our lives
The picture we see
Will be the one we have painted,
Stroke by stroke,
Day by day,
And framed in intention.

The Lure of the Morn

The lure of the morn,
When birds sing
And roses greet the day,
Petal by petal,
And all creation welcomes
The morning sun.

The lure of the morn,
When babes wake and cry
And mothers hold them close,
When children stir,
Slow to rise,
Eager to play.

The lure of the morn,
When the dew is fresh
And branches flower
And welcome breeze
And honey bees –
That is when my soul stirs,
Awakens to another day,
Thanks Him
For His endless gifts.

The Poet Sheepishly Replied

The poet was asked,
"How many poems have you written?
Have many verses have you penned?"

The poet responded humbly
That he had written many.
The poet was then asked,
"From where your inspiration?
What of ideas lost?"

The poet gently responded,
"They come and go,
Each one a beauty fair,
A maiden true.
Some stay and linger,
Others flee and vanish,
Forever lost."

The poet was then asked,
"What then of inspiration,
The stream of ideas?
Will your pen run dry?
Will the page remain bare?"

The poet reflected momentarily
And then sheepishly replied,
"Fortunately,
Each one of these maidens,
Each one of these beauties fair,

Has at least one sister,
And, as they are always welcome,
They visit quite often!"

The Sound of One Heart Loving

"The sound of one hand clapping"
Intrigues me not,
Neither will it ever.
Such paradox is for others
To ponder, unravel.

The sounds I seek
Are of another sort,
Transcendent, resonating sounds
That ring loud as church bells
And true as the song of the whip-poor-will,
Sounds of such pure intent
As to thrill cloud and sky,
Reach to the heavens,
Be celebrated in the Great Beyond,
Sounds that traverse hill and vale,
Soar high above mountain peaks
On irrepressible spiritual winds,
Even as softly wafting summer breezes,
Ballerinas of the skies,
Dance across meadows flowered in gold
And prairie grasses dressed in green
To honor the sun.

The sounds I seek
Are more melodious than meandering streams
Rushing down a mountainside
Romancing faithful, steadfast banks,
Their long, caring arms forever outstretched,

Sounds that surpass
The cooing of nesting doves
Or the enchanting melodies of nightingales
Inebriated with the intoxicating
Wine of the rose
Mystically poured from wineskins
Of matchless fragrance and inimitable beauty,
Sounds that emanate from the heart
And fly from soul to soul
On the wings of joy and love,
Hope and justice,
Prosperity for all peoples,
All God's children.

The sound of one heart beating
In love for another,
O how sweet this sound!
It throbs and pulsates
In the bosom of brotherly love
Within the enlightened body
Of one humanity –
One in origin,
One in purpose,
One before its Creator.

It is the blessed sound
Of a heart irrepressibly beating
For love and betterment,
Friend and stranger,
Family and neighbor,
A sound answering the call
Of ancient melodies,
Supernal, holy,

Proclaiming a oneness adorned in resplendence –
Colors light and dark and tan
From the Eternal Palette
Of unfailing beauty,
Colors brushed by the Master of Magnificence
With love, meaning and purpose.

It is a sound
Known to every creed and across every clime.
It is a sound that humbles songbirds
Singing upon the branch of love songs
And swallows swooning away
In mystic tones
As they tell their tales of love.

It is a sound
That wafts from heart to heart
And soul to soul,
A sound heard across the ages
And cherished by the cherubim.
It is the sound of the story of love,
True, unsuppressed, timeless,
Exquisitely recited,
Perfectly told.

The sound of one hand giving,
This, too, I love to hear!
What might it be,
If not a concerto of generosity
Featuring harp and lute of caring souls
And orchestral strings of pure, selfless intent
Played on the stage
Of well-wishing for all humankind?

Or perhaps,
It is a symphony composed by saints,
Sought by seers and played by angels,
Its orchestrations reverberating
Bosom to bosom
In heavenly tones of loving kindness?

Such are the sounds I seek!
We have but to listen
To hear their resounding tones
Of spirit and serenading love,
Born of the heart
And played in the soul,
Each note as clear and purposeful
As a clarion call and the ringing of bells,
And, assuredly,
More lovely
Than even the loveliest
Of windblown chimes
As they plead undying fealty
To enamored,
Courting winds!